EXPEDITION
Ark of the Covenant

EXPEDITION
Ark of the Covenant

The Young Messiah's Meeting
at The Throne

DR. JIM RANKIN

XULON PRESS

Xulon Press
2301 Lucien Way #415
Maitland, FL 32751
407.339.4217
www.xulonpress.com

Revised 2023

Printed in the United States of America.

Paperback ISBN-13: 978-1-5456-1263-7
Hard Cover ISBN-13: 978-1-5456-1461-7
Ebook ISBN-13: 978-1-5456-1386-3

It's been a lifetime of travels, sometimes into the valleys, but always returning to the higher peaks. Through it all, my wife has been there by my side, even when it didn't make sense at first. This is dedicated to a love unmatched on this earth, Sherri, whom has been there through it all. And to our children, Shayne, Austin and Skyler, their faith in me has been a blessing. To those whom the Lord has put in our path to complete each step and discovery. Finally, to the great I Am for the guidance, answers to prayer, and for the love that is eternal.

Contents

ACKNOWLEDGEMENT

THIS PROJECT HAS BEEN part of an amazing adventure in my life. It has been a journey that has been full of intrigue, amazement, revelation, and many tears in order to complete. Stepping back and looking at it all now, I have come to realize that it would not have been possible without the assistance of many individuals along the path of my life. There are so many that have played an intricate part in preparing me for this trek that it would take another book to thank them all. I will just say that I regret that I am unable to share each of their names within this acknowledgement, but I want them all to know that their reward is yet to come.

I must extend thanks to a few who really have trusted me to not only accomplish this life- changing task, but also to meet the challenges that have been given to me throughout my life. To these people I owe my most humble gratitude: my wife Sherri for her unmatched love and encouragement in every victory and defeat; my wonderful children Shayne (encouraging from above), Austin and Skyler for their incredible endurance to stand behind me at any cost; my parents, Ronald (who is with the Lord) and Betty for their belief in me from the very beginning; Dr. and Mrs. Verlis Collins for their prayers and trust in my ability to reach the world for Christ; and the many others whom have entrusted their prayers my way.

Because of these people, and many others, my life has been filled with prayer, support, and guidance along every journey I have already taken. But the adventure isn't over, and I now thank those I haven't yet met, who will be a part of future explorations. This journey is just the beginning, and God only knows where His next exploration will lead. But I do have the surety that wherever He leads, I will follow.

Praise and Testimonials:

THROUGH THE EXCITEMENT OF the release of Jim Rankin's book, '*Jesus In Ethiopia*' several years ago, and the success in the transition and education of not only those in the western world to see the truth and discoveries documented within its pages, but to see the results of its release in Europe and Ethiopia, was God lead from the start. Not only did it become a best-seller, it began to transform the teaching, and the education in schools, colleges, and many other avenues in the process.

Expedition: Ark of the Covenant is not just a follow up to *Jesus In Ethiopia*, but a replacement, highlighting new facts, discoveries, more evidence, and truth behind what the first book only touched upon. Much is the same, while is much more has been refined, added through the continued research, and revealed through even more ancient finds.

That brings us to the overwhelming testimonials and accolades Jim Rankin received because of the research and evidence that was shared to the world through this book.

"This is incredible work...the discoveries are just amazing with God's favor on you, but the work you're doing for the Lord through this is, leaves me speechless, and that's not easy to do. He's a modern-day Indiana Jones with a Bible in hand."

—Bobby Schuller (Pastor-Shephard's Grove Church, Host of TV's *Hour of Power*)

"It is just fascinating information. It makes one realize the closeness to the times that are coming."

—John Rhys-Davies (Proclaimed Actor)

"I appreciate your (Jim's) compassion and dedication to your faith...the entire adventure is exciting and enriching."

President George W. Bush
(*43rd President of the United States*)

"He's like a modern-day Indiana Jones, but this guy carries a whip in one hand and Bible in the other...truly amazing, and he continues to be blessed with more and more mysteries being revealed to him."

—Mother Love (Actress, Author, Host of *Mother Love Show*-LA Talk Radio)

"This is just amazing to me. It proves the Bible, and really encourages us to fulfill our duties laid out in the Scriptures."

Dan Fisher (Former Oklahoma Congressman, Pastor-Liberty Church, *Black Robe Regiment*)

"Fabulous, this is just fabulous. To see what God is revealing to you, and then to see what he is allowing you to do through these wonderful people, is just so precious."
— Jan Crouch (The late Mrs. Crouch-founding member of TBN, *Trinity Broadcasting Network*)

"I was amazed! I learned a great deal, and it was so inspiring."
— Jimmy Mellado (President of *Compassion International*)

"I love this history, and what it all represents. Especially the Ethiopian Jews, and what they mean to the times still to come."
— Raleigh Washington (President of *Promise Keepers*)

"I really just don't know what to say...this is just the most compelling and heart stopping, and let me add fascinating research I've ever seen. It just makes me want to cry. It's just overwhelming."
— Dr. Gwen Ford (Host of *I Believe* TV Talk Show)

"What more is there to say. This is just amazing information, and it all fits in-line with the Bible. The revelations to Jim to get to this point have been undeniable, and it just floors me to the accuracy of confirming what the Bible says and beyond."
— Gary McSpadden (Pastor-Faith and Wisdom Church, Formerly with The *Oak Ridge Boys*, *The Statesmen*, *The Imperials*, *Gaither Vocal Band*, and former co-host of TV's *PTL Today*)

Now let your adventure begin!

Chapter 1:

WALKING ON HOLY GROUND

Moses and the Burning Bush engraving

THE MOUNTAIN BLAZED AS if it were on fire, glowing
in the night, and engulfed in clouds mysteriously consuming
it. It was the holy mountain of God, Mount Sinai. This was a
place that no one had stepped foot upon unless called upon
by God Himself. One day long ago a man named Moses was

chosen by God to scale this mountain to encounter Him. A voice commanded, *put off thy shoes from off thy feet, for the place whereon thou standest is holy ground,* (Exodus 3:5). One can only imagine the whirlwind of thoughts that must have spun in Moses' head as he apprehensively approached a most awe-inspiring sight. Before him, as he came closer to the Voice that uttered those words atop the burnt mountain, he saw a bush burning brightly, though not being consumed. The Voice was that of Jehovah God, barreling out His instruction and commands upon the one who was chosen to lead the enslaved people from bondage in Egypt, back to the Lord-ordained Holy Land. The thought of hearing those words, *for the place whereon thou standest is holy ground* must have brought Moses to a gut-wrenching halt as he quickly removed his sandals, realizing that he was in the presence of God Almighty.

Moses had an enormous task on his shoulders, because no one would have ever imagined that he would have been the one chosen to fulfill this command. From having been cast out from the land of Egypt as a once thought prince, to his speech impediment that would surely hamper relating the message from God, we see the continued pattern in the tradition of the Lord to choose the most unlikely to complete the most miraculous. Moses' humble beginnings bring him from a family of Hebrew slaves, to the royalty of the Pharaoh's palace, to the holy ground on the top of Mount Sinai. In his own right, Moses took quite a journey culturally, emotionally, and spiritually to reach the point that God had entrusted in him to carry out His plans. That phrase will ring true, *for the place whereon thou standest is holy ground*, as we continue our own modern-day adventure as well. As a matter of fact, it will be a phrase that will send shivers down my spine as we travel throughout this journey. As Moses stood with God upon the mountain, one can only imagine some of the discussions that took place. The Bible only gives us a glimpse into that conversation. So much knowledge, wisdom, and grace had to be placed upon Moses during his time on Mt. Sinai. It's mind boggling to know that God entrusted this man so much that He would keep him upon this mountain for quite some time to teach him.

Let's start this story from the time Moses came down from the mountain from *Holy Ground* with God. Following the biblical flight-line, the traditional location of the Helena site of Mount Sinai on Jabal Musa in the Sinai Peninsula in no way matches any account shown clearly in the Scriptures. At the base of this mountain is Saint Catherine's Monastery, along with a collection of theme park-like souvenir hounds offering their wares to gullible tourists looking for anything relating to their visit to the mountain. Years earlier my former brother-in-law even made the trip to this location (during a stint in the military) and fell to the belief and frenzy that this was the holy mountain of God. Tourists and pilgrims for centuries have been lured into this belief and, in some odd way, have come away fulfilled with a false fullness of the spirit within.

Helena, the mother of the Roman Emperor Constantine, chose this location as Mount Sinai. Helena ventured out with a strong coalition of soldiers in pursuit of artifacts and biblical locations, as she felt her calling to be. In many cases, force

3

was exerted to achieve this purpose. With many of the Helena claims, there are no factual or logical trails of substance to bring reliable truth to many of these sites or relics. Regardless, her unsubstantiated claim of Jabal Musa being the traditional site has been drawing millions of worshippers throughout the centuries paying homage to more of their faith than of the location. Even biblical scholars aren't completely sold on the idea that this is the true Mount Sinai. You will find this as fact when examining biblical maps found in most everyday Bibles. In your search in many of these maps, you will most likely find a question mark next to the location of Mount Sinai. That leads us, or should lead us, to look further and to discover a more accurate biblical description.

The most likely site is reported by biblical explorers such as Jim and Penny Caldwell *(ref. 2)*, Robert Cornuke *(ref. 3)*, and others as being located in Saudi Arabia, just as the Apostle Paul accurately distinguishes in the book of Galatians 4:25; *For this Agar is mount Sinai in Arabia.* Amazingly enough, from the natural land bridge in the Red Sea that the Israelites would have crossed (Exodus 14 and 15), to the bitter springs of Marah (Exodus 15:23), to the twelve wells, or springs, and seventy palms of Elim (Exodus 15:27), to the mount itself, Jabal Alaz, is near evidence enough. For decades, anyone trying to reach this restricted Saudi area, an off-limits military and archeological site, you would have seen warning signs that trespassers will be prosecuted based on an antiquities law of the country. Today, this site has been opened to special groups to visit and see the evidence. Here, you would find enough evidence to stand up in a court case at this location. Discovered at this site was a stone altar engraved with Egyptian cows, similar to those of the Egyptian gods Hathor and Apis, as found in Exodus 32. Of course, this Scripture also states that the people ordered Aaron to shape a golden calf and place it on the altar they had built. As in Scripture, we notice that there was more than one calf, noting the many calves engraved in the altar in Saudi Arabia, and matching Exodus 32:4, *after he had made it a molten calf: and they said, These be thy gods, O Israel.* That explains the altar for the golden calf in addition the calves etched into the stone itself *(ref. 2)*.

Also located are the barriers around the mountain described in Exodus 19:12:

> *And thou shalt set bounds unto the people round about, saying, Take heed to yourselves, that ye go not up into the mount, or touch the border of it: whosoever toucheth the mount shall be surely put to death.*

The twelve columns and sacrificial altar seen in Exodus 24:4:

> *And Moses wrote all the words of the LORD, and rose up early in the morning, and builded an altar under the hill, and twelve pillars, according to the twelve tribes of Israel.*

As shared in the Scriptures, a cave is located in the face of the mountain where Elijah took shelter on Mount Sinai in 1 Kings 19:13:

> *...when Elijah heard it, that he wrapped his face in his mantle, and went out, and stood in the entering in of the cave.*

But one of the most stunning features is the coal black rock that only can be found capping this mountain. It's a very unusual black rock that, when broken, shares the same rust orange colors inside as found consistent on the rest of the rock common to the area. This coal black covering may help explain the Scripture in Exodus 19:16-18:

> *And it came to pass on the third day in the morning, that there were thunders and light-nings, and a thick cloud upon the mount, and the voice of the trumpet exceeding loud; so that all the people that was in the camp trembled. And Moses brought forth the people out of the camp to meet with God; and they stood at the nether part of the mount. And mount Sinai was altogether on a smoke, because the LORD descended upon it in fire: and the smoke thereof ascended as the smoke of a furnace, and the whole mount quaked greatly.*

Split rock of Moses discovery by Jim and Penny Caldwell
(Photo courtesy of Penny Caldwell, Split Rock Research)

Then, with Jim and Penny Caldwell's find of Moses' split rock nearby, this piece of evidence puts the final stamp on the case. The evidence that the Caldwell family discovered while at the split rock, including the obvious dried water trail leading from the rock into the valley and the flaked erosion beginning from the bottom, gives the overall impression that the water was gushing from the base of this huge stone monolith, and completely brings to life the incredible find of all of these explorers at Mount Sinai *(ref. 2)*. This rock was split when Moses took his staff and slammed it against the stone causing water to gush into the valley below, as seen in Numbers 20:7-11:

> *And the LORD spake unto Moses, saying, Take*
> *the rod, and gather thou the assembly together,*
> *thou, and Aaron thy brother, and speak ye unto*
> *the rock before their eyes; and it shall give forth*
> *his water, and thou shalt bring forth to them*
> *water out of the rock: so thou shalt give the*
> *congregation and their beasts drink. And Moses*
> *took the rod from before the LORD, as he com-*
> *manded him. And Moses and Aaron gathered*
> *the congregation together before the rock, and*
> *he said unto them, Hear now, ye rebels; must*
> *we fetch you water out of this rock? And Moses*
> *lifted up his hand, and with his rod he smote*
> *the rock twice: and the water came out abun-*
> *dantly, and the congregation drank, and their*
> *beasts also.*

With this discovery, we have to rely more strongly on the evidence than with the tradition that Moses actually went up to meet with God on this holy ground and descended back down to his people carrying the Ten Commandments of the Lord. It was at this place that God commanded Moses and his brother Aaron to construct a box made from acacia wood, or shittim wood, and then overlaid it with gold to contain the commandments. They were then instructed to build a solid gold lid with two cherubim angels atop with their wings folded and facing the center point of the lid known as the mercy seat of God. This wasn't just a lid; it was the throne of God, the only place since God walked in the midst of the Garden of Eden that He would actually appear on this earth. This would be the place where God would dwell during His appearance on the Day of Atonement in the temple or tabernacle.

As Aaron became Moses' spokesperson, and eventually the high priest to carry out the meeting with the Lord in the tabernacle during the trek to the Holy Land, the Ark of the Covenant became possibly the greatest and most mysterious artifact in history. Its power was unstoppable and the miracles that surrounded it were beyond human understanding. From bringing down the massive stone walls of Jericho to parting the waters of the flooded Jordan River, the Ark of the Covenant was a holy artifact that was worshipped by all who believed in God, and feared by everyone during the time of Moses and beyond. Even to touch the Ark would bring death because of its holiness and the separation between God and sin. Even now, a replica of the Ark of the Covenant is an object that is highly revered and thought to be a holy artifact because of what it represents to many faiths. In some faiths around the world, in their churches you will find a replica of the Ark inside a Holy of Holies. If, for any reason, that replica would be removed from that church it would literally mean that the church would lose its holiness and become deconsecrated as a result.

In the ancient times, on the Day of Atonement, the high priest would go to the Tabernacle to prepare himself before entering the tented structure. The priest would first spiritually have cleansed his body of sin and then would go into prayer for the forgiveness of sin of the people. It was a literal spiritual removal of the sin before he presented himself in front of God in the Holy of Holies. This same ritual continued into the time of Solomon's temple, and even up to the time of Jesus' ministry. The high priest would have to physically wash himself completely and then he would be dressed in seven holy garments which was representative of honoring the coming Messiah. He would wear a long coat, linen breeches, and the robe of the ephod colored blue with golden bells sewn into the hem. The most important part of his dress was the ephod with the outer material made of fine twined linen representing the Messiah's purity; with gold representing Christ's deity; with purple representing Christ's royalty; with blue representing heaven; with scarlet, which showed the coming sacrifice of Christ. On the front were the stones of the twelve tribes of Israel which represented the burden of the people carried on the shoulders of the high priest, just as Christ carries our burden on Himself. Finally, the priest would add the girdle, the breastplate, and the turban, or mitre, which he would wear upon his head.

Properly attired, the high priest would enter the Tabernacle with the bowl of sacrificial blood and pause in the first chamber before the table of shewbread, altar of incense, and the golden candlestick lampstand. He would purify himself once again, as he did with the outer cleansing before entering the Holy Place. Inside the Holy of Holies, the priest would again go into a solemn issuance of prayer and repentance for himself and the people, before removing the covering upon the Ark. He would sprinkle the blood of the sacrifice directly on the Mercy Seat (the Throne of God) for cleansing where God Himself would sit, and then on the floor beneath for cleansing where the soles of God's feet would be planted. God's desire since the Garden of Eden was to dwell with us, but our sin has kept Him from us. That's why so much care had to be taken to cleanse even this small area for the arrival of the Lord Himself. If for any reason, God didn't accept the plea of the high priest for forgiveness, the priest would be struck down by the power of God through the Ark. He would then be pulled out by the rope that was attached to him if the people didn't hear the bells jingling anymore from inside the tabernacle. If all went as planned, God would forgive His people and bless them. Finally, following the beginning rituals, God would then give additional instruction for His people or to prepare them for whatever was to come. The high priest would go into prayer once again before covering the Ark of the Covenant and the Mercy Seat until the next meeting, or for travel.

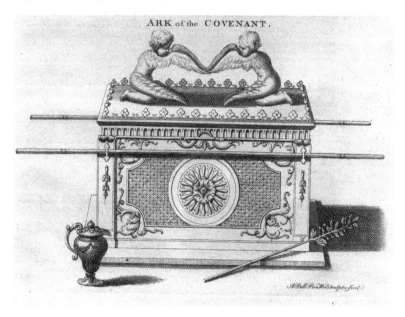

Ark of the Covenant, Andrew Bell copper plate engraving
from the 1797 Encyclopedia Britanica

The Ark of the Covenant would take its rest inside the Tabernacle tent along the journey of Moses and the people of Israel on their trek to the Holy Land. Eventually Solomon constructed the temple in Jerusalem that was thought to be a permanent home to the Ark of the Covenant. Sin, defilement, and destruction of man, however, eventually put an end to that original plan. The Holy of Holies was considered so deified that only the specifications that God laid out could be housed within that place. Anything else would desecrate the room and God's presence would be removed. The Levites were extremely careful and protective over the Ark and the Holy of Holies in order to carry out their appointment as the overseers of this holy object. Even a hint of turmoil or invasion and the Levites would remove the Ark of the Covenant and retreat with it to safety.

Just as God told Moses to remove his sandals as he was about to walk on *holy ground*, the same was true for the high priest as they entered into the Holy of Holies. There was nowhere that projected the divine nature of God's presence on this sinful earth than in that chamber where the Ark of the Covenant rested, and between the Cherubim on the Mercy Seat, which was literally the throne of God. The Ark of the Covenant and the Mercy Seat carried with them a heavenly force not to be reckoned with.

From this point, the story of the Ark in the Scriptures is far from over. The sacrificial need for the Day of Atonement and the dwelling of God on the Mercy Seat, continued until the fulfillment of the Ark of the Covenant's purpose came in the form of Jesus Christ on this Earth. The sacrificial ceremonies were a necessity throughout the ages. Then, as we know, Jesus became the law, and carried them within Him, thus becoming the sacrificial Ark. The fact is, *holy ground* plays a divine role throughout the ages. From the Garden of Eden, where God dwelled with Adam and Eve, to Mount Sinai, where Moses knelt in humble fashion on holy ground, to the Holy of Holies in the Tabernacle, and in the Temples themselves, God's desire to be with us has never ceased. That's why those words on *holy ground* play such a prominent role in our journey and in our everyday lives in search of the truth of the meeting between the Father and the Son.

Chapter 2:

THE ADVENTURE BEGINS

LOOKING BACK, THE ARRIVAL in Ohio was a bit of a shock to this Central Floridian. With my father retiring from the Air Force, he wanted to return to his home in Southwest Ohio where he began his journey twenty years earlier at Wright Patterson Air Force Base in Dayton. Knowing that the family would have to make their way on ahead, we began our journey northward months before he would be able to finally retire. A year later the family on my father's side started an annual reunion in the backwoods area of Southwest Ohio, far from the city, into the hilly woodlands. This was a land I wasn't familiar with and to be quite honest, not too sure of either. There were no swamps with alligators, the accent of the people was unfamiliar, and they dressed a little different, according to Florida standards. To reach the site of the reunion, we had to travel across many backroads and finally arriving at the little old trailer my grandmother lived in. We drove around the trailer and my dad told me to get out of the car and pull the latch on the old gate and open it so he could drive through. This entered into a cow pasture and then onto a rugged grass and dirt path along a hillside back into the woods.

One of my earliest recollections of my grandmother, who was well into her eighties, was her sharing stories of being a little girl in the late 1800s and jumping into the twentieth century. She was a kind woman, but very strong willed in her age. On our very first day in her small trailer, my uncle had caught a huge snapping turtle in a nearby pond. My grandmother, cane in her left hand and a sharp machete in the other, stepped onto the turtle's back and with one whack, took off his head. I'll never forget her saying to my dad and uncle, "Skin him and bring him in to boil." I could tell quickly that she was a survivor, and I knew this woman was someone I wanted to know better. She had been through many struggles in life and had the battle scars to prove it. But, at the same time, she had a passion to share her life with the ones she loved. Stories of seeing President William McKinley and attending the Buffalo Bill Wild West Show proved this woman had even more stories to keep a young explorer like me wrapped up for days. One of her most intriguing stories that she shared with me was about the contents of an old wooden box containing the keys to a trap door at the home Reverend John Rankin, one of the initiators of the Underground Railroad in Ripley, Ohio. In this wooden box, she revealed a collection of documents that Reverend Rankin had written, including papers that he would give the slaves after they had made their way across the Ohio River. It also included a layout of his land and a couple of hidden locations used for the movement of slaves. (One of those places I had tried to inform the historical society at the site of his home for nearly thirty years and then one day someone finally dug with the historical society of Ohio and they found an underground chamber. Not knowing what it was, they simply filled it up and went on. Wow, the history that is lost!) Unfortunately, after the passing of my grandmother, the box and its contents disappeared, another example of neglected history.

After visiting my grandmother, we drove on this worn and rutted driveway into the back country, to a nearly washed away dirt path, into a wooded area where the families would gather and pitch their tents, build up wood for an evening fire, and set up card tables for endless tournaments of euchre. For this adventurous young boy, I wanted nothing to do with that. There was wilderness to explore and the boring thought of planting myself at a euchre table was not part of my adventure. They played their game all day long, it seemed like to me, or as I would hear often, "until the cows come home." So, in the midst of their entertainment, I would disappear into the forest, not return until it was time for the late evening dinners. A growing boy had to eat, and I wasn't about to miss the evening meals which always consisted of homemade fried chicken, mashed potatoes, and usually corn bread. It makes me hungry to recall that delicious childhood memory!

During my adventures, I would swing on vines, slide down shale covered embankments, and build forts to hide away in. I would pretend I was a combination of Tarzan, Daniel Boone, Jim Fowler, Davy Crockett, and Evel Knievel all wrapped into one young boy. I was always open to adventure, and I had the imagination to create whatever the surroundings presented me with. One afternoon, while sitting near the creek bed up against an oak tree, I started digging in the dirt and saw a series of little stones that appeared to be fossilized Cheerios laying arranged in a perfect circle. To my surprise, there were dozens of them in a pattern right next to the tree. As I kept digging I came across four arrowheads in the same area, as if they had been buried there in something that had rotted away over the centuries. Quickly, I began to realize that these weren't ancient Cheerios, but some type of bead or fossils carved as beads for ceremonial and decorative dress for ancient Indians.

With this new-found discovery, I decided to try my luck in another area about fifty yards from this particular spot, where two creeks forced into one bigger one. Again, Indian beads, arrowheads, and even an ax head this time. Had I by accident stumbled across some type of former ancient American Indian village from centuries earlier? Over the next six years, I filled coffee cans with beads of all different sizes, arrowheads so perfect that they would still take down a large deer, ax heads, a staff head, and pottery. Eventually, it became obvious I had been excavating an ancient Indian village that had been lost in time. My brothers didn't have much of an interest in the excavation, but occasionally my sister Debbie would join me in the hunt. After my grandmother passed away the reunions in this place would gradually dwindle, and I felt it best that this area remains untouched until some other day. As a matter of fact, nearly fifteen years later I would bring my own children to this site to explore and dig up some of those incredible artifacts. Still today, this remote area in Ohio remains the way it was when I was a boy. As for me, other than crabbing off the beaches of Florida and enticing alligators in the swamps, and now exploring and discovering an ancient Indian village in the woodlands of Ohio, this need for adventure and the desire to explore has never gone away.

Needless to say, my life has been a wild adventure, fulfilling nearly every dream and passion that I've ever had. I've met and worked with some of the most noted celebrities over the ages, while traveling from coast to coast in my professional pursuit of the thrills of life. I've shared the stage with some of the entertainment businesses top performers, stood in the presence of presidents; jumped a few motorcycles, and built a great relationship and prayed regularly with notables such as Evel Knievel, Carl Perkins, and many others. Even slept in Elvis' house! Despite these thrills, my dream for historical adventure was still my unrequited passion.

A FAMILY GETAWAY WITH A TWIST

It was a steamy morning in late July 2009. My family and I had made a quick getaway from Ohio to the Great Smoky Mountains in Eastern Tennessee. One of my specific rules when taking road trips is to make very few restroom stops so we can reach our destination and enjoy our time, rather than spending extended time on the road. So, in order to keep the thought of having to stop out of my wife's mind, she would bring pillows and blankets and nestle into her seat and sleep for most of our trips. When we traveled to Tennessee, everybody knew that our first stop would be at the Tennessee Welcome Center at the border with Kentucky. From that point, we didn't stop again until reaching the Smoky Mountains which was about an hour and a half ahead. At the end of our five-hour journey we finally took the exit off of Interstate 40 to Sevierville, Tennessee. After driving through Sevierville into Pigeon Forge, the home town of Dolly Parton, we took the short, wooded roadway to Gatlinburg, our home for the next three days.

When we arrived, the town of Gatlinburg was bustling as always. The traffic was backed up as usual, and folks from all over made their way into this mountain play land. We pulled down a side street turning right and crossing the concrete bridge over the river to our hotel. After checking into the hotel, we fulfilled tradition and made our way down to the strip in Gatlinburg to see what's old and new. Once we made our way back to the hotel, we enjoyed a swim and a relaxing splash in the hot tub before finally retiring for the night. I was beat, tired from the earlier drive and worn out from walking up the Gatlinburg strip. The heat and humidity had physically drained me, and it was time to call it a night. It didn't take long for my eyes to close and my mind to lapse into a state of dreams.

Within a short time into my calm sleepy slumber, I had a startling wake up around 3:00 a.m. that sent me flying straight up into a catch my breath upright position. My wife just sighed and turned the other way oblivious to the dramatic event that was about to reshape our lives. I heard a voice, a whisper, or even a thought that came over me for the need to research the

Ark of the Covenant of the Old Testament. Nothing else, just the Ark of the Covenant! Sure, I had knowledge of the Holy Ark of God, but never had I felt compelled to research it more fully. After all, my favorite film was Raiders of the Lost Ark, and my wife always looked at me as Indiana Jones himself, as I would take the family off on some far-fetched adventure. But this awakening was the simple thought of the Ark of the Covenant and nothing more. I was clueless on this one, but knew that there had to be some meaning behind it. It was too plain not to have some purpose beyond my understanding. My wife simply said, "Lay back down." So, I laid my head back down, and off to sleep I went for a few more hours.

After we awoke, I walked out on the balcony to take in a breath of fresh morning mountain air. I could tell right away that it was going to be another steamy day that was common in this area. We loaded up the family and left Gatlinburg for Pigeon Forge and joined thousands of others on a tram to Dollywood Amusement Park. While we were riding, that thought came to me again about the Ark of the Covenant. Yes, the Ark that carried the Ten Commandments! The Ark that Moses, David, and Solomon had so reverently celebrated and protected. What was I supposed to do? Listen, I'm in the Smoky Mountains with this need to research this incredible piece of history. Thoughts of Raiders of the Lost Ark and the movie The Ten Commandments consumed me. Why did I have this urge, this strong desire? Was it just a feeling, or was it a calling?

PROPHETIC PAINTINGS AND TRUMPETS

Here's where things really became interesting. Later that day we visited an art gallery in Pigeon Forge featuring a local painter who was very well known for his incredible work. His name was Spencer Williams, and his work in the window was beautiful. I walked in and found him sitting at a canvas next to the large plate glass window working on his next masterpiece. We began talking about his work and he described his portrayal of a Roman guard in a local passion play. I told him that I was a pastor and about our ministry with a great opportunity in the area we lived to reach out to so many in need. Mr. Williams continued to paint as others entered the store to admire his work. His assistant, I assumed, wandered over and said, "Let me show you something I think you'll really like. This is why you really came in here today." Puzzled, I followed her around the corner where she stood in front of a beautiful painting. Gazing up, she said, "This is really why you came in here today isn't it?" I stood mutely at this large painting on the wall. A beautifully painted face of Christ was in the upper left-hand corner with a bold Lion of Judah lying on the ground with a crown, and a large scroll next to Him. Then, prominently taking center stage, was the Ark of the Covenant. It wasn't an hour before when this overwhelming urge had come over me once again to begin research on an amazing historical artifact that consumes a great deal of the Scriptures, and it was now somehow beginning to consume my life. And now, a woman I had only just met takes me to view a painting featuring the

Ark. I scoffed it off as coincidence, and moseyed my way out of the shop to visit a friend named Larry Stinson who owned a jewelry shop next door at the time. Larry and I had connected a couple years earlier in another twist of fate, and our friendship snowballed from that point on. After exchanging a few ideas, we hugged and I went on my way to find my wife, Sherri, gazing through the area's many shops.

We left Pigeon Forge and ventured back to Gatlinburg, Tennessee, just a few miles from the busyness of its neighboring city. We made a left turn onto highway 321 and traveled to the Arts and Crafts district of the Great Smoky Mountains. Here you'll find pottery shops, painters, and a variety of incredible talents that attest to the ability of the artisans. As we stopped at one conglomerate of gift shops, my wife wandered off into a shop with purses in the window, while I had more of a purpose to my shopping detail. I made a couple stops with my boys into a magic shop, and then a concrete statue yard before going ahead and visiting a shop hoping to pick-up something for my wife, since our anniversary was the next day. As I looked around, the owner approached me and said, "I might have something you're interested in over here." Not wincing, I turned and followed her to a rack of a few uniquely handmade necklaces. She selected one necklace in particular and said, "This is the one you're looking for." Of course, in my infinite wisdom, I smugly thought that to be a quick-sell to the tourist line and said, "No, I'm looking for something for my wife and I don't know if she would like that." From nowhere came the words that shocked me as she replied, "In the Bible

22

in the book of Numbers, chapter 10, I believe, is the story of when God called on Moses to make two trumpets out of silver to call the people to His tabernacle. This is a handmade necklace of those trumpets of Moses." My eyes grew wide as I was thinking, "Here we go again." We are standing in the mountains of Tennessee and I have a woman whom I have never met before telling me of trumpets of Moses to call people to the tabernacle that housed the Ark of the Covenant. I began to wonder if these trumpets were actually calling me. I wasn't sure but I quickly said, "Thank you, but I'll keep looking." She replied without haste, "No, I mean this is for you. Please take it, it's the reason you came in here today." Bewildered and baffled, she placed the necklace over my head and around my neck. I stood there momentarily dazed and uttered a mild "thank you," and turned for the door with the necklace of the trumpets of Moses dangling around my neck, and many thoughts racing through my mind. I turned back to her in the doorway as she nodded and told me to enjoy my time in the Smoky Mountains.

I thought that was surely enough for the day, but it didn't stop there. Two hours later, as the night sky began to shine, and the downtown lights of Gatlinburg were brightly illuminating the streets, we decided to walk the strip and do a little shopping. The humidity had subsided and the temperatures were much more bearable, which made for a very pleasant evening. Austin and Skyler were on their own adventures in Gatlinburg as my wife and I walked the sidewalks, people watching and gazing at store displays. And then, very loudly, the theme song of *Raiders of the Lost Ark* began to belt out of one of the mini golf locations inside a building. I turned quickly and the man working the adventure golf attraction put his hand on my shoulder and said, "I don't have the Ark, but would you like to play some golf, buddy?" "What?" I exclaimed! He turned his sights to other passersby in his attempt to entice other customers, but my heart was pounding. The song and the comment left me a little shaken, but it was just another confirmation that God had something in the works that He was preparing me for. I quickly grabbed my wife's hand and moved away as fast as I could. We continued to move on and enjoy the beautiful evening together. Sherri wanted to know why I picked up the pace and scurried away so quickly. I shook it off as though I didn't notice anything and the topic was quickly forgotten. The next day it was time to leave the Smoky Mountains and begin my research. What was God trying to tell me? Where would this journey lead me? I knew it wasn't going to be an easy study but I also knew it would be more than just another adventure. I knew this one may not be what I think it might. Something had changed for me during this visit to the mountains, and little did I know what God had in store.

Two years after this journey, and the events in which you are about to read had been completed, I returned to the shop where the painter sat in the window and shared with him my story, and how it all began that day with a visit to his shop. I let him look at my manuscript and read about the events that had taken place with the woman asking me to follow her to the back of the shop. As he read, he began to cry, and sat the manuscript down. He turned, left the showroom and went alone into the back. After he returned, he looked at me and said, "Jim, I've never had a woman like that working in here. That was not of this place." Stunned, just as he was, I shook his hand and walked out of his store without saying another word. Sherri and I felt as though we should drive back to the area where the woman had given me the necklace of the trumpets of Moses. As we pulled up to the area where the bustling shops were, just two years prior, we were speechless to find the entire complex abandoned. We were now completely convinced that God had His hand on this journey from the beginning, and we were just being prepared for the events to come. With all that said, the adventure you are about to embark on has been nothing short of a miracle, and we're confident you will soon agree.

A GOD-ARRANGED MEETING INITIATED

After returning from the Smoky Mountains, I began to seriously research the Ark of the Covenant. It was funny because I thought I knew all I needed to know about this ancient artifact. I had studied the Ark at Bible college, and was under the impression that I had all the answers. How wrong I was! I started where all searches should start, in the Holy Scriptures. Genesis, Exodus, Deuteronomy, Numbers, 2nd Chronicles, it seemed like the more I searched the Scriptures the more I found myself almost visualizing what Moses, the Israelites, Joshua, David, Solomon, and Hezekiah were going through on each trail of their journeys, battles, and prayers. I knew there was more to my search that I didn't understand, at least not yet. I studied about Moses' desire to serve the Lord and the frustrations he went through with the Israelites, and their constant disobedience. Then I went to Joshua and his faithfulness to follow along with the commands of the Lord who dwelled between the cherubim on the Mercy Seat of the Ark. King David was an example both on how to treat and not treat the Ark of the Covenant, and the consequences that must be paid when God's instructions are not followed. I studied the Israelites' Ark worship instead of their faithfulness in just trusting God. Then I moved on to Solomon and his struggles, and then to Hezekiah's prayer at the foot of the Ark. I extensively looked into the all-important Mercy Seat of God upon the top of the Ark and the Cherubim that kept guard over that Seat. This sparked another desire for study on the many conspiracy theories of the disappearance of the Ark. The theories were so numerous that I started to lose count of them. I became enthralled with the overall power that the Ark possessed, and how incredible it must have been to witness its strength. God's presence through the Ark slew armies and no one could touch it, let alone look at it except for the high priest in the Holy of Holies. I continued to research for days on end to find out every last little bit of information I could on the Ark of the Covenant in the Bible. It was so important to my study, but I still needed to figure out what God had in store for me.

This continued from August until early December 2009. Our church had planned an outing to the Creation Museum in Northern Kentucky to see their spectacular Christmas display called the Christmas Town. After the outing, we stopped off at a pancake restaurant for a late-night bite to eat where another conversation began. It was suggested to me, "Jim, why don't we start a study on some of the true biblical sites in the Bible that you are always talking about, like Noah's Ark and stuff? Since you love this historical stuff, why not share some of it with us?" "Sure, why not? I'll start working on it Monday," I responded. I went home and began researching DVDs on some of the most reliable discoveries of true sites of the Bible in recent years. The Garden Tomb and Mt. Sinai were high on the list, as I found programs that I viewed earlier on TBN, History Channel and Discovery Channels. I located a variety of videos, and one in particular was Mountain of Fire that featured explorer and author, Bob Cornuke. I called the phone number to order the video, and Cornuke himself answered the phone. He said he was leaving on a documentary shoot in Malta to continue his discovery of the anchors from the lost shipwreck of the Apostle Paul, and told me that he would be happy to send us the DVD. That was the entire conversation and it simply ended right there.

My search for biblical discovery DVDs continued, as did my research in to the Ark of the Covenant. In January 2010, I prayed about men in our church to help me build a replica of the Ark for an upcoming Sunday morning message. For some strange reason, I felt the replica would serve to demonstrate my message. The men I chose to build the Ark started to assemble it on a cold January evening. I didn't tell them what we were doing before-hand, but I simply gave them each instruction and diagram on what they needed to build. My friend Terry Erwin built the box and lid, and I let him on the project ahead of time so he would have it ready for us. He was a great woodworker and I was confident that he could pull it off. When we arrived at the church, Terry had already done his work and left it sitting on a table in a small museum area that we had constructed. The others began to arrive. When I brought out the drawing of my plans, each of the men took a step back, gulped, and said, "We are building what?" The others all had a specialty that they needed to complete for the project. Over the next week, we worked nearly every weekday evening, hiding the ark each night to keep it out of sight of anyone else in the church. Finally, on January 25th, 2010 the replica was completed as I put the last coat of gold flake paint over it and prepared it for Sunday's service. It was beautiful. I didn't show the men the completed project because I wanted it to be a surprise to them as well. When they last saw it, the ark was still just a box with trim around it. Tim Moore and I took it from there and added the angels, poles, and paint to give it the final look. It was amazing, authentic in nearly all respects.

The next morning was another typical day. I got up early and headed out for my daily routine, but I found out a couple of hours later that this was to become anything but a normal Tuesday. My phone rang, and it was Bob Cornuke on the other end. He had returned from his journey to Malta and seemed very tired as he began to speak to me. But what he had to say to me was shocking and somewhat prophetic. He said, "Jim, during my trip to Malta I couldn't get your name off my mind. I am planning an expedition on the trail of the lost Ark of the

Covenant and I feel like you're supposed to be with us." My first reaction was "WHAT?" He went on to say "I don't know what it is, but for some reason you are supposed to be on this journey with us." I didn't know what to say. I was taken back and surprised. Listen, this would be a dream come true, but it was a little odd to me that he would ask this with all that had happened up to this point, even the completion of the Ark, which had nothing to do with this phone call, just a day earlier. I told him that I would have to pray about it and that's what I did. For the next twenty-four hours, I prayed and talked with Sherri about the trip. She was just as amazed as I was, but not overly surprised. She had just said three days earlier that she felt our greatest adventures were still to come. I felt like donning a brown fedora, pulling out my western style whip hanging in my shed, and throwing on the DVD of *Raiders of the Lost Ark*. I love those adventure films, and that's all that was running through my head. With my exploration past and the compulsion to study the Ark, I thought I knew where this journey was about to go. I picked up the phone and called my friend Terry Erwin and told him about this call. He quickly said that he was shocked to a point, but really wasn't surprised and had a feeling that God had more of a plan than just building a replica Ark that I told him about.

The next day Cornuke's wife, Terry, called me and said that after talking to Bob, she felt my wife Sherri needed to be with me on this trip. After hanging up, my phone rang again and it was another Terry. This time it was Terry Erwin, the only one who really knew this whole story from Gatlinburg to the building of our replica Ark. He said, "I've been thinking a lot about this guy asking you to go on this Ark expedition and I really feel that if you go, that Sherri should be with you." I paused, swallowed and finally said, "That's really strange, Terry, because just five minutes ago, Cornuke's wife, who is also named Terry, called and said that she felt Sherri should go as well." He concluded immediately, "Then it sounds like you have your answer." Later that day Sherri and I sat down and I relayed about the phone conversations to her. She was one hundred percent with me, a surprise considering she knew nothing about what we were getting ourselves into. Ironically, this call came the week we finished the Ark replica, two days before my birthday, and five days before my message to our church on the Ark of the Covenant. I began to realize very quickly that our lives were about to change and head a direction that I had never imagined. Although somewhat hesitant, I was excited about this very quick turn of events. This was becoming very evident that we were about to enter into a new and thrilling chapter in our lives fulfilling a life-long desire to explore the world in search of adventure.

Finally, the Sunday arrived when I was to give my message on the study of the Ark. I had a dramatic scene set up as if it were devised for a movie set. After our worship music, and during the offering, I disappeared into an office behind the altar and quickly changed into some *Indiana Jones*-looking clothing. I ducked out the back door and snuck around the side of the building. I had forgotten that the snow hadn't been shoveled on that side, and I was jumping through drifts up to my waste. The lights grew dim in the auditorium and an eerie music started to play. I came up the aisle and made my way to a pedestal near the stage. On the pedestal was a very small replica of the Ark in which I did the dramatic switch with a bag of sand. I made my way up the aisle and doors to the auditorium burst open. Instead of a large rolling boulder barreling toward me, my mother in her motorized wheel chair blasted through the door as I appeared to struggle to get away on my way to the stage, barely making an escape. The congregation erupted in laughter but still amazed at the mini-adventure in front of them. Then I was attacked by two treasure seekers whom I had selected earlier from the audience who were quickly defeated with a crack of my whip. It was quite the scene and brought a great deal of excitement and laughter to start off the service. As I spoke about the Ark, I told the congregation the Ark looked just like this little replica that I had in my hand. Then I stepped back and said, "No, it looked more like this one." The doors burst open, and again as music played, four of the builders of the replica were dressed in Hebrew looking costumes and carried the Ark upon their shoulders with another leading them down the aisle. Cell phone cameras came out of nowhere as everyone wanted to capture the moment and a memory of this incredible full size gleaming gold box. The message was full of intrigue, surrounded by the Holy Spirit which led a young lady at the end of service to the altar and gave her life to Christ. Then before everyone left, I announced that Sherri and I had accepted the opportunity to go on this journey, and everyone erupted in applause anticipating this incredible opportunity.

This decision launched a series of speaking engagements and fund raisers as we prepared for our journey, and it was such a blessing to see the efforts of so many. It wasn't just an excitement for Sherri and me, but a building of excitement for many others as well. Everyone wanted to be a part of the expedition by helping to make it all happen. In my own mind, I was excited to see all of this, but couldn't help but wonder what else was in store for me. Somehow, I knew that it wouldn't stop with just being involved in an expedition. I knew that God had more in mind when He started us on this journey some six months earlier. One lady said, "I'm not surprised, your life is an adventure every day." And honestly, it truly has been, but this one may be the setting for the rest of our lives. Time will tell.

Chapter 3:

THE BETHLEHEM CALLING

IT'S ALMOST A WHIMSICAL thought, that a young man and his wife had to make such a long, tiresome journey to the village of his heritage in order to be included in a census for taxation. Today, we tend to run from the taxes, but at this time, that's exactly the opposite of what young Joseph and Mary did as they traveled to Bethlehem.

> *And it came to pass in those days, that there went out a decree from Caesar Augustus, that all the world should be taxed. (And this taxing was first made when Cyrenius was governor of Syria.) And all went to be taxed, every one into his own city. And Joseph also went up from Galilee, out of the city of Nazareth, into Judaea, unto the city of David, which is called Bethlehem; (because he was of the house and lineage of David:) To be taxed with Mary his espoused wife, being great with child.* Luke 2:1-5

The young couple who made that commitment, knowing that Mary was not only *great with child*, but great with The Child, began this long journey that was sure to be full of hardships and criticism. This miraculous journey was not one that the couple really could predict the outcome of, but they knew that it was something that had to be fulfilled. Ridicule was sure to follow them, and trials were sure to plague them during this long trail they were about to travel. Either way, they knew what they had to do, and were on their way to fulfill both the decree of Caesar and the prophecy of the birth of the Savior. This wasn't just going to be a trip to Bethlehem, but a life-long struggle that would begin with a short journey. Their minds must have been in a whirlwind during the trip. Why them, and what was the next step? As we know, the greatest journey for them was yet to come.

From today's perspective, to travel from Nazareth to Bethlehem would only take a couple of hours to complete the one hundred-mile trip in a car. Over two thousand years ago, it would have been a long journey, and it was a mandatory request by Caesar Augustus that all were to return to their city of lineage for the calling of the census. This is a time when they would have most likely made the journey on donkey, camel, or horseback, and even with that, only one of them could ride while the other walked. With an internet search, or if you visit this particular region of Israel, you will note a couple different types of terrain in this land today; You either battle the desert sands, or you deal with rocky paths and mountains. Either way, it wasn't easy by any means with rough trails, a scorching sun by day, and much cooler temperatures that left them shivering in the night. A two-hour journey for us today would have easily been at least a nearly week-long trip for a young man, his pregnant spouse, and their belongings.

Most indications show that this couple likely made their pass through the River Jordan Valley. While starting in Nazareth, approximately 1,200 feet above sea level, this trek would have descended quickly, and most likely would have taken them across the river a couple of times before arriving in Jericho. They possibly would have passed by Waddy Kelt, where King David had herded his father's sheep. This area, filled with canyons and deep valleys, is where many believe David wrote Psalm 23. From here, Mary and Joseph would have mostly likely ventured from the lowlands to the high mountains of Mount Olivet, and either into or around Jerusalem.

Another recent archeological find in this area uncovered a church that contains a rock believed to be where Mary rested with Joseph on their way to Bethlehem. As in many of the traditional sites in Israel, Jordan, Egypt and other parts of this region of the world, they are marked by traditional churches, commemorating what is believed to have been the locations that either Mary or Jesus rested upon, touched, or it is noted as a site where some historical event occurred. There is no real way to tell, but the likelihood is that something was recorded to have taken place there at one time in history. And even though scholars want tangible proof, many times the tradition passed down through the ages may be the only proof we will ever have, and our discernment will have to lead us to make the qualitative decision of whether to believe it or not. Finally, Mary and Joseph would have arrived in the area known as Bethlehem Ephratah to complete the first leg of a life-long journey for God.

Shortly after their arrival in Bethlehem, Mary went into labor and gave birth to the King of Kings in a so-called stable. We must look at this a little closer in order to gain a true perspective on the truth of their accommodations, because the Greek word for "inn," in this case, is actually *kataluma (ref. 4)*, which is more understood as a guest room. It's important that we understand what this actually would have been during this ancient time period. Since this journey was due to a decree sent out among the entire Roman Empire, the couple would have, more than likely, attempted to stay with relatives. But with the slower journey for them because of Mary's pregnancy, they would have probably arrived much later than others in the family, and were turned away from the guest room and sent to the lower end of the home where the animals most likely stayed at night. Considering that many homes were built into and above caves, the family would often bring the animals into the lower end of the home during the cooler nights. Soon after this arrival, Mary went into labor and gave a miraculous birth to Jesus, the Savior of the world, in a humble setting in a far-away town.

Around the time of the birth of Christ, trouble was brewing in nearby Jerusalem. King Herod knew of the birth of a king, but was not aware that it was The King. Due to his pagan beliefs and lack of truly spiritual knowledge, he was more concerned of the threat to his overall power and his throne. That was obvious from his next decree. With the inability to find this king who had been prophesized, the jealous Herod, realizing the wise men whom he had asked to return to him with information on the whereabouts of the child, weren't coming back to give him the information he requested, sent out an order to murder all male children from the ages of two and under.

And being warned of God in a dream that they should not return to Herod, they departed into their own country another way. Matthew 2:12

Then Herod, when he saw that he was mocked of the wise men, was exceeding wroth, and sent forth, and slew all the children that were in Bethlehem, and in all the coasts thereof, from two years old and under, according to the time which he had diligently inquired of the wise men. Matthew 2:16

It was near this time that Joseph had a visit from a Holy being;

And when they were departed, behold, the angel of the Lord appeareth to Joseph in a dream, saying, Arise, and take the young child and his mother, and flee into Egypt, and be thou there until I bring thee word: for Herod will seek the young child to destroy him. When he arose, he

> *took the young child and his mother by night,*
> *and departed into Egypt...* Matthew 2:13-14

This was without a doubt a frightening call upon Joseph and Mary, to say the least. Remember, this was a couple who had just traveled from Nazareth to Bethlehem upon the order of Caesar Augustus. We know that this wasn't immediately after the birth of Christ because we see that the Scripture tells us that the wise men came to a house and visited with a young child. No longer was Jesus a baby:

> *And when they were come into the house, they*
> *saw the young child with Mary his mother, and*
> *fell down, and worshipped him: and when they*
> *had opened their treasures, they presented unto*
> *him gifts; gold, and frankincense, and myrrh.*
> Matthew 2:11

So, from what we can gather from the Scripture is that Jesus was near the age of two when they began their next journey. As we see in Matthew 2:14, Joseph was instructed by the angel to take Jesus and Mary and flee from this area, completely beyond their comfort zone, into unchartered territory for them. This was a beginning to a miraculous and untold adventure that prepared Jesus for all that was to come.

Scripture brings Joseph once again face to face with an angel sent from heaven:

*And when they were departed, behold, the angel
of the Lord appeareth to Joseph in a dream,
saying, Arise, and take the young child and his
mother, and flee into Egypt, and be thou there
until I bring thee word: for Herod will seek the
young child to destroy him. When he arose, he
took the young child and his mother by night,
and departed into Egypt.* Matthew 2:13-14

Herod's soldiers were on their way to slay the children two
and under, and the angel warned Joseph to pack up this family
and begin an exodus from the land they knew and loved. Rather
than remaining hidden in their homeland, the holy family would
go to a land notorious for their worship of idols before massive structures erected to receive their worship. One can only
imagine the fear and confusion that gripped Joseph and Mary
as they crossed over to this mysterious land of Egypt with Jesus.

Without any doubt, Jesus knew exactly what was to come.
He was not only escaping the slaughtering blades of the Roman
soldiers, but He was on His way to meet with God the Father
in another far-away land. During this miraculous journey, the
prophecy that God's Son would enter into this land and idols
would fall to Him was only the start of events to come. This
family was about to venture into the unknown with their personal possessions bundled up, including the gold, frankincense,
and myrrh from the wise men. All they had was possibly a
donkey and their own company to count on. Isn't that the trade-
mark of a family? They had each other, and that's what really

matters, not forgetting that they also had the Lord of Lords in their presence. Really, when you think about it, what more do we really need for our own unknown journeys but Jesus?

Chapter 4:

THE GREAT
JOURNEY BEYOND

NO LONGER WERE JOSEPH and Mary a family from Nazareth, but now they were considered fugitives on the run from the evil king Herod and his fearless army. Although the Scriptures are silent about this portion of the life of Jesus as a boy, there are plenty of oral traditions and written documents that follow a very well-defined path of the holy family in the ancient land of Egypt. There are many credible historical documents that follow this path, traditional stories passed down through time, and many writings that journey through this topic thoroughly. Some of these writings come from lost, or hidden, records of Gospel writer Mark when he ministered in Alexandria, Egypt. In this research, we will take you through a historic path that was more of a journey to guide us along the trail to somewhere already planned out, rather than to escape from the situation that awaits them if they don't heed to the call to move on. By now, I hope I have your attention to move further. Again, John 21:25 states:

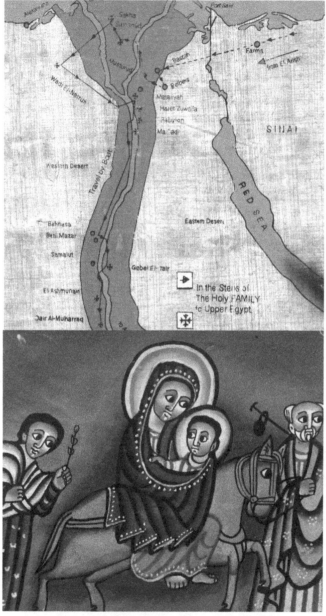

Top: Map of holy family trek coming into Egypt.
Bottom: Ethiopian 5th century painting of the holy family
entering Ethiopia

And there are also many other things which Jesus did, the which, if they should be written every one, I suppose that even the world itself could not contain the books that should be written. Amen.

John tells us that there was much more that took place in the life of Jesus that wasn't included in the Scriptures. That's obvious since we have nearly thirty years that are untold in Jesus' life since His birth until He began His ministry on Earth. And you will also find it ironic that it is John that makes these comments for what you are about to read in this book.

The Bible gives us what we need to become a Christian in faith, to turn our lifestyle to become more Christ-like, and to learn what is needed for nearly every topic that life has to offer. Then there are other non-canonical historical books that contain further clarifications not found in the Scriptures, and were not needed for the application of righteousness in our lives, but could have been inspired or passed down through time to give us additional reference to what we were given in the Bible. With that said, this exodus journey was more for the preparation of the ministry of Jesus to offer His followers until His eventual return. This adventure was not necessarily intended for Mary and Joseph, but for Jesus to prepare Himself for the introduction of His deity to the world. It's an amazing thought that nearly 2,000 years since Christ was born, we are just now realizing that there was so much more to this King of Kings and His relationship with His Holy Father. We would be given glimpses of this many times in the Scriptures, such as in the Garden of Gethsemane in Matthew 26:39;

> *And he went a little further, and fell on his face, and prayed, saying, O my Father, if it be possible, let this cup pass from me: nevertheless not as I will, but as thou wilt.*

And then we would see it several times while Jesus was on the cross in Matthew 27, John 17,19, and Mark 15. It's best said in Luke 23:34, 46;

> *"Then said Jesus, Father, forgive them; for they know not what they do."* Luke 23:34

> *"Father, into thy hands I commend my spirit: and having said thus, he gave up the ghost."* Luke 23:46

We also see the reference to the deity of God the Father resting in Christ throughout the gospels, as well. It will also show us that the discussions Jesus had with His Father in the gospels were not based on a short-term relationship, but rather it was the climax to the education that Jesus was taught earlier in His life, and seen in Scriptures such as:

> *For I have not spoken of myself; but the Father which sent me, he gave me a commandment,*

what I should say, and what I should speak. And
I know that his commandment is life everlasting:
whatsoever I speak therefore, even as the Father
said unto me, so I speak. John 12:49-50

THE BEGINNING OF THE JOURNEY

Egypt was a different world for the holy family. They were entering into land where pagan gods were in the majority, and their faith in Yahweh would be put to the test many times during this journey. The vast land of Egypt and its mighty empire bowed down to gods such as Baal, Astarte, Amun, Mut and Khonsu. These gods were worshipped in various locations throughout the empire of Egypt, including the area known as Luxor, the Valley of the Kings. This is evident from the number of temples that can be seen in this once mighty city still today. The one thing that the Holy family had going for them, other than God in the flesh traveling with them, is that the cultural acceptance of Egypt would be a welcoming relief as they made their trek through this country. Although there are many mentioned noted possible locations that the holy family may have passed through, we will only focus on the ones that have a documented significance to their path and journey.

Today, the land of Egypt is mostly visited for their great pyramids and statues to the pharaohs of the ancient past. However, a keen interest has emerged in the last few years to document the trail of Jesus traveling throughout this land. This has brought a different relevance to the interest in Egypt, one that is really well-defined. Each area where the holy family passed, you will find churches or some type of memorial to identify and recognize their appearance in the village.

From all indications, it appears as though Jesus, Joseph, Mary, and a previously unknown figure on this retreat (one that we will examine later), made their entry into Egypt from the north-east region in the modern-day location of Rafah. This area can be distinguished because of a lone ancient sycamore tree that is said to have been dated to the time the holy family visited while passing through. It is important to note that many of the first few locations that the holy family passed through were brief visits because of the threat of Herod's soldiers still on the search for Jesus.

After passing through Rafah, they moved onto the city of El-Arish for another brief respite. This is a city nestled on the banks of the Mediterranean Sea, and the reference to their entering and exiting El-Arish is barely mentioned in any ancient writings. But we know they would have had to pass through here to move further on.

Although there were a couple other locations they may have possibly passed through, their last location in this area was in Pelusium, or Tell El-Farama. This is a place that was once a busy port-city, but now is a village of ancient ruins, including numerous Roman churches. Again, this would have been a short stay for them, as they moved on to escape the approaching soldiers of King Herod. Their journey continued as they moved on to one of the branches of the Nile River in the city of Tell

El-Basta, which they probably passed through before resuming their flight through Egypt *(ref. 5)*.

Al-Mahma, the bathing place as it is known, was their next stop. In Al-Mahma, ancient history tells us that Mary bathed Jesus in this town. In a newly restored church, built in the 12th century, you will find the place where this event was to have taken place. Al-Mahma was not the most pleasing place to the holy family though, as we will find in many of their stops along this path. It was unsafe, and Mary and Joseph knew they had to protect their Son. They quickly gathered up their things and headed to the north to a friendlier environment in Bilbeis. *(ref. 6)*

PROPHETIC DESERT ENCOUNTER AND FRESH SPRINGS RISE

The holy family ventured on, crossing the Nile into the western desert, as they headed for the village of Scetis, known today as Wadi Al-Natrun. On this path, in the desert, a prophetic encounter would take place, as laid out in the 1st Infancy Gospels (Chapter 8:1-8), and in Coptic writings as well. This was a migrating ground for thieves. Knowing this, Joseph and Mary made the choice to attempt to pass through this area during the night. During this quiet attempt to move through, they came upon two thieves asleep along the road, and attempted not to awaken them. The thieves, Titus and Dumachus, were awakened and startled by the unexpected passers-by. Dumachus attempted to do what he did best, and tried to rob the holy family. Titus, realizing the company they were in, pleaded to Dumachus to let them pass without altercation. Dumachus continued, and again Titus, fearful of what might be put upon them from God Himself, pleaded with him by offering him gifts to let them pass. Mary recognized the kindness of Titus and said, *The Lord God will receive thee to his right hand, and grant thee pardon of thy sins*. After the encounter, Jesus turned to His mother and said, *When thirty years are expired, O mother, the Jews will crucify me at Jerusalem; And these two thieves shall be with me at the same time upon the cross, Titus on my right hand, and Dumanchus on my left, and from that time Titus shall go before me into paradise (ref. 7)*. This foretelling of the two men on the cross with Christ was a prophetic beginning that would come to involve many more foreseen predictions to come during their flight through this strange, but beautiful country.

After a short visit in Wadi Al-Natrun, they continued on to where Cairo is located today. They moved to the east bank of the Nile River to the city of Heliopolis. The name Heliopolis is taken from the Greek name for the Pharaonic city of On in the ancient times. Located today just outside of Cairo, it is called Ein Shams, when translated means "the eye of the sun." From here they traveled to Matarieh where a very unique event was recorded to have taken place. As the holy family took shelter under a large sycamore tree, Mary sat next to the tree, and from out of the ground a spring of fresh water started flowing. If you visit Matarieh today, you will still see what they claim to be as *Mary's Tree*, an ancient and decaying sycamore tree said to be the tree where she sought shelter with Jesus *(ref. 8)*.

STATUES FALL AND IMPRESSIONS IN STONE

The trek for the holy family continued to the south with stops in Al-Zeitoun, Al-Zweila and eventually to Babylon which today is known as Old Cairo. Local history states that when Jesus entered the town, the idol statues fell to the ground as prophesized in the Old Testament:

> *Behold, the LORD rideth upon a swift cloud, and shall come into Egypt: and the idols of Egypt shall be moved at his presence, and the heart of Egypt shall melt in the midst of it.* Isaiah 19:1.

This upset the people in such a way that the governor of the territory attempted to find them, and have Jesus killed. Writings show that Jesus, Joseph, and Mary hid in a cave, which today carries some unique and distinctive marks to memorialize their visit. Today this cave is below the church of Abu Serga (or Saint Sergius). After their escape, the holy family continued onto Maadi, to the south of Old Cairo, and then took a ferry boat across the river to Memphis, which was once the capital of Egypt. They boarded a boat from here to the town of Ashnein Al-Nassara where you will find a monastery on this site today where a deep well is located that allegedly supplied the holy family with water. Four days later, they journeyed on to a site known today as *the house of Jesus* or Abai Issous (present day known as Sandafa). From here they stopped in Samalout and then to the east bank of the Nile River to Gabal Al-Tair, known as *the mountain of birds.* The family took up shelter in this spot in a cave where a church now rests above. As the historic writings show, while in this place a huge rock began to fall on the family, but Jesus held up His hand to stop its landing. Legend has it that this rock contained the embedded handprint of Jesus. Even though similar to the footprint in Sakha, this relic has been lost to the ages *(ref. 9).*

THE COPPER IDOL FALLS

Continuing on, just south of Gabal Al-Tair, there is an acacia tree whose leafy branches are said to have swept the ground and turned up as the holy family passed by. For this reason, the locals in that area call it the *Worshipper.* Continuing south, the family arrived in Bir Al-Sahaba, where they crossed the Nile River once again. Eventually they came to Hermopolis Magna where a very kind man helped shelter the family. Taking them in, he risked a great deal of trouble because of his kindness. The reason behind the trouble resulted from the huge copper statue that fell when they entered the town. The people believed that evil spirits were in that idol, and when it collapsed and broke, the spirits were let loose. The priests were angered by this, and the family was forced to move out of Hermopolis Magna quickly. The kind man that sheltered them, on the other hand, was in a great deal of trouble for showing compassion to Jesus and His family *(ref. 10).*

DEATH FOR HIS FAITH AND PALMS THAT BOW

The holy family moved on into the town of Al-Ashmounein, which brings us to an unfortunate end for one man proclaiming the deity of Jesus as He entered the village. A young man named Wadamun, who was from the village of Armant and knew upon seeing the young Jesus in front of him that He was sent by God, made it known by declaring the deity of Jesus as they passed through the village. Because of his act of worship, Wadamun was put to death by the priests in the village. Although we see many martyrs later in the New Testament, this very well could have been one of the first to sacrifice his life by proclaiming Jesus as the Messiah.

Again, the holy family would leave this hostile area and continue their venture to the south arriving in the Dairout Umm Nakhla, *the mother of the palms*. As we saw earlier in Gabal Al-Tair, when Jesus passed through the town, the many date palms that lined the streets were believed to have bowed to Jesus as He passed by. In this area, there is a very peculiar set of palm trees that again seem to be bowing in their struc-ture, unlike many others surrounding them along the pathway still today.

Abu Haneis was the holy family's next stop as they crossed back over the Nile River again to the east bank. Here they stopped for a period to quench their dire thirst from the belting sun and crystallized desert sand. At Abu Haneis, the well that quenched their thirst was named Sahaba. This is translated *cloud*, thus named to the credit of Mary *moving like a swift cloud* in search of water for her Son. The reception here was much more encouraging than many of the previous stops along their trek. With that welcome, they decided to take some time here and rest on a hill that is still named today Kom Maria. Nearby, a church still stands commemorating this visit by the holy family, the Church of the Holy Virgin *(ref. 8)*.

HOSTILITY AND WELCOME

Eventually their trek continued southward, crossing the Nile once again, and arriving in the town of Daitout Al-Sharif, or Philes in ancient times. With word spreading who this child could be, hostility grew, and the priests became anxious, inciting the people to drive the holy family from their village. Again, as they journeyed onward, another hostile encounter took place in Al-Qusseya, where they were driven out because their godly claim cast fear upon their pagan worship lifestyle. It seems ironic that even when Jesus was a boy, they were driving Him out of their lives. Unfortunately, the world seems to continue to do the same still today.

Finally, the holy family arrived in Meir, where they were received with open arms. After a short stay, they traveled to al Muharraq, or in ancient times Mount Qussqam. In Egypt, they actually stayed at this location for the longest period of time, for six months and ten days as noted in historical writings. We must also note that because Muharraq is not the farthest region to the south that it is claimed the holy family visited, we must assume that the time period they spent here may have been split between a visit to and from their final destination to the south. It is reported that after they passed through Muharraq and were welcomed, that Mary wanted to return to this city. The word Muharraq means *burnt*, because the grasses in the area were set on fire to enable the farmers remove vegetation and to plant crops *(ref. 8)*. In this town, you will find what is reported to be the first church built in Egypt over the cave where the holy family took shelter during their stay. The Coptic Christians never consecrated this church because they claim that it didn't have to be blessed because Jesus consecrated it by His presence there. This was a favorite location of Mary, and the family considered this home for a period of time.

From al Muharraq they continued southward to Dayr el-Maymun where the villagers believe that Jesus blessed the village as He passed through there. Continuing south, the holy family ventured into Wadi Al-Rayan and took up shelter in a series of caves. These caves were known to house hermits, and were also heavily used as a perfect hiding place in later years for Christians dodging the Roman persecutions. They then ventured by Sawada, and to Asena, Dayr al-Barsha, Dayr Abu Hinnis, Buq, Assiut, and finally their farthest point in Egypt in Dayr Rifa. This Egyptian village contains an incredible cave church that was built later to recognize the holy family's visit there *(ref. 9)*. Many in Ethiopia believe that this was the final stop for Jesus before continuing to Ethiopia for the prophetic meeting at Lake Tana.

THE JOURNEY HOME

Although nearly every bit of evidence points to the holy family living in Muharraq, I have to believe that since they enjoyed their stay there, that after returning from the future prophetic meeting, they returned to the safety of Muharraq to wait for the calling to return home. Egyptian writings claim that the holy family stayed in Murharraq until Joseph received the calling by the angel to come to Israel. I can't help but question why Joseph would take his family so far south, through hostile surroundings in many cases, to then be told that it was time to come home. There had to be a purpose for such a long journey. Herod's soldiers in no way could have followed them that far to the south. Jesus would have known that, and God wouldn't have put them through the struggles of traveling if He didn't have another purpose for them. This is also one of the clues that led me to question why they would travel so far to the south knowing that there would be a long return home. What was the purpose of this journey southward?

Best-selling author Paul Perry shared with me many of the highlights of his exploration to Egypt to study the flight of the holy family. But when asked if this was the last stop, for him it was, because this is where his research stopped for his study. Paul's book, *Jesus in Egypt (ref. 8)*, is without a doubt, a great source for research on the topic of the trek of the holy family into Egypt. To his credit, his research was specifically about the holy family only in Egypt. That's why nearly every source discussing the flight of the holy family stops in or around Muharraq before heading back to Israel.

That really fueled my inquisitive mind and enhanced my questions of, *why*? Why such a long journey, and what were they still running from? I couldn't get past the thought that God would send Jesus and His Son's earthly family on such a treacherous and long journey. It didn't add up to me. But, tradition controls so much of our thought process. Little did I know my questions were about to be answered.

The Coptic writings tell us that the long journey for the holy family home was ready to begin. Later you will learn of the family's movement into Ethiopia, so after leaving Ethiopia they would have traveled back to Assiut, and then ventured back to Muharraq. It is there the writings tell that Joseph received the calling of the angel for them to return home.

> *But when Herod was dead, behold, an angel of the Lord appeareth in a dream to Joseph in Egypt, Saying, Arise, and take the young child and his mother, and go into the land of Israel: for they are dead which sought the young child's life. And he arose, and took the young child and his mother, and came into the land of Israel.*
> (Matthew 2:19-21)

It's believed they sailed the Nile River to Memphis and docked at Al-Badrashein. They would have passed through Maadi and Heliopolis and then through the desert, until they arrived in Nazareth where Joseph felt it better to go, rather than return to Jerusalem, because they feared Archelaus, son of Herod, the new ruler. As they came out of Egypt, it again fulfilled the prophecy of Hosea *(ref. 5)*;

> ...*then I loved him, and called my son out of Egypt.* (Hosea 11:1)

Many believe that when the holy family left Egypt, they may have joined up with one of the many bands of merchants that traveled the desert. The reasoning behind this is that their fear of Herod's son seeking Jesus and to use the safety of the caravan. These caravans also traveled a much easier and safer route. The road home through Judea and Samaria would have been extremely rough. The caravans traveled a road known as Via Maris, or the *Way of the Sea*. This road connects Egypt and Damascus and enabled the merchants to freely travel to all areas in Middle East *(ref. 6)*. This trek would have taken years to complete, and with ten years missing from Matthew 2:13 to Luke 2:47, we see that much more happened within this journey than what we learn from the Bible alone.

TO THE LAND BEYOND

The first question that the critics will pose is that the Scriptures say nothing of Jesus going any farther than Egypt during the retreat from Herod's soldiers. That's true, but we must also realize that those same Scriptures give us no insight into where Jesus went in Egypt, or why is was so long before we heard of Him again in the Bible. The Scripture only tells us that they went into Egypt and nothing more. One man quizzed me on the ability of Jesus as boy. "Do you believe Jesus could perform miracles and received His later godly power as a boy?" At that moment, I became more defensive in my response than I should have. I was more shocked than anything that someone would think that Jesus was all of a sudden "awarded" His godly ability when He matured. Or maybe God would snap His fingers and Jesus would magically be given the title of "Son of God." When that question arose, I was still somewhat unclear about some of the things I had been shown on my journey, and needed more time to research further. Yet, spontaneously I blurted, "Yes, I believe Jesus Christ was God in the flesh from the moment He was conceived, but just not given all He needed at that time." This brings me to the Scripture in Isaiah 7 that tells us that the coming Messiah will be given, and taught what He would need to know to finish His miraculous task:

Therefore the Lord himself shall give you a sign; Behold, a virgin shall conceive, and bear a son, and shall call his name Immanuel. Butter and honey shall he eat, that he may know to refuse the evil, and choose the good. For before the child shall know to refuse the evil, and choose the good, the land that thou abhorrest shall be forsaken of both her kings. Isaiah 7:14-16

THE LAND OF THE BIBLE'S ETHIOPIA

Let's now go beyond Egypt and drop down to Ethiopia, which was the area below Egypt at the time of Jesus' trek into this foreign land to the holy family. More specifically, let's look at the ancient land of Ethiopia, and its relation to the Bible, with a further glimpse into both the desolate and beautiful features of this land. First, Ethiopia is a place like I have never experienced before. Shrouded in tradition, mystery, love, poverty, growth, and beauty; Ethiopia combines the wonders of the ancient times with some of the luxuries their world has to offer. The capital city is Addis Ababa, where you see incredible poverty contrasted by the wealth of the palace of the country's president, the embassies of many of the world's powerful countries, and a boom in economic growth. However, we will not be focusing on this part of the Ethiopia. This is a land that connects the feeding point of the Nile River to Egypt, but it's also a land built around survivors in time and element. The people are some of the most loving people I have ever experienced in my travels, while they are in many cases suffering from HIV, tuberculosis, malnutrition, alcoholism, and a variety of other horrible conditions. But that's not all of them. One thing is true; they have an abiding faith for the most part.

Let's take a look at that faith. To look at this correctly we have to go back to Noah and his family. After the great flood waters had receded into their banks, Noah's sons and their wives were told by God to disperse and replenish the earth.

And you, be ye fruitful, and multiply; bring forth
abundantly in the earth, and multiply therein.
And God spake unto Noah, and to his sons with
him, saying, And I, behold, I establish my cov-
enant with you, and with your seed after you.
Genesis 9:7-9

They packed up their belongings, and began their journeys
to the outer parts of the Earth. Shem, Noah's oldest son (and
the one that Jesus allegedly descended from) went out with
his family to what is now Israel and the area of Northeastern
continental regions. Japeth took his family to Asia Minor, and
modern-day Europe and began their new life in that region.
Then, Noah's youngest son, Ham, began his roots in the area
believed to be between Ethiopia and Egypt today, with his
family spreading across Africa, into Canaan (which is Saudi
Arabia) and Western India. Ham's son, Mizraim settled the
land of Egypt, while his first son Cush (Kush or Ityopis) estab-
lished Ethiopia and beyond into the Great Rift Valley region.
Another of Ham's sons, Phut, settled the area by which we
know today as Libya.

Looking at this region, you will find the oldest location near
the Aksumite Kingdom in Northern Ethiopia today. It was here
that during the time of King Solomon, who reigned from 970-
930 BC, received a visit from the Queen of Sheba according
to 1 Kings 10:1-13. Enamored by her beauty, the King surren-
dered to her charms, and the Queen conceived a son whose
name was Menelik. Much tradition surrounds Menelik and his

involvement with the Ark of the Covenant. One of those traditions say that the king's son came back to visit his father in Jerusalem, and Solomon showered his returning son with favor and riches during the visit. The people of the kingdom also generously welcomed him back to his father's kingdom. This undue attention greatly concerned the priests, and they went to Solomon and warned him that Menelik would have to go because of the danger of the people's devotion to him. Solomon agreed but stipulated that the first born of those in the kingdom of influence, who were encouraging for Menelik to leave, must go with him to Ethiopia. In this order, the son of the high priest removed the Ark, and many other items, and stole them away. During their travels to the Axumite Kingdom, Menelik was informed of the items that accompanied them.

Another theory speculates that the son of Solomon stole the Ark of the Covenant from the Temple of God, and replaced it with a copy. He brought the Ark back to Ethiopia as a gift to his mother. Neither tradition carries any merit whatsoever, because we can see the holy Ark remained in the temple of Solomon long after his death. We see that nearly two hundred and fifty years after Solomon the Ark still remained in the Temple during the time of Hezekiah's reign.

And Hezekiah prayed before the LORD, and said, O LORD God of Israel, which dwellest between the cherubims, thou art the God... (2 Kings 19:15)

Nevertheless, Solomon had appointed Menelik the King of Ethiopia after he returned to Jerusalem to receive a blessing from his father. This is the most commonly accepted belief of how Ethiopia received Judaism, which soon spread throughout the country.

The Falasha Jews, or the black Jews of Ethiopia, began to practice this form of Judaism, but they were secluded with only the Pentateuch (the first five books of Moses), and centered their belief solely on these writings. Axum (Aksum), Ethiopia became a great city and a mighty kingdom which had a direct tie to the trading routes of the Roman Empire with the connection of the Red Sea at the eastern banks of Ethiopian's northern coast. As the most common accounts have been reported over the centuries, two Syrian boys shipwrecked there and became slaves. After gaining favor with Emperor Ella Amida, these two boys began to teach Christianity to the king. After the king's death, his son Ezanus (or King Ezana) took over the mighty throne around 300 A.D., and the Christian faith began to spread. Ezana appointed one of the boys, Frumentius, who was now an older man, as the bishop of Ethiopia. In approximately 305 A.D. as the bishop, Frumentius began to spread the Christian belief throughout the land of Ethiopia. He even led King Ezana to the Christian faith. Frumentius was reported to have been taken, upon his death, to the island of Tana Kirkos located on Lake Tana, and buried there. Later, his body was moved to Daga Stephanos, a nearby island. King Ezana also plays another role of importance to Axum history, which we will review more closely in chapters to come *(ref. 11)*.

AXUM, ETHIOPIA: CITY OF THE ARK

Massive solid stone obelisk in the ancient city of Axum, Ethiopia

Now that we have looked at the arrival of Christianity in Ethiopia, let's look at this country today. The northern region of Ethiopia is made up of a variety of villages and cities with spiritual and historical significance. Keep in mind, even though many of these locations are seeing incredible growth, they are not the same that we in the western world are accustomed to. Like one of my great friends in the tourism department of Ethiopia said to me, "T.I.A., Mr. Jim. This is Africa, this is not America." In many cases the facilities have seen better days. This is not to say that there aren't great places to stay, eat, and see, but one must keep in mind that it's Ethiopia, and it's a very special place. One of the best examples of this is the city of Axum, where many of the mighty rulers reigned, including the Queen of Sheba (Makeda or Saba), King Ezana (Ezanus), King Kaleb, and others. One of my most amazing discoveries during my visit is that much of the ancient kingdom is still buried under centuries of sand, dirt, and rocks. Nearly every year the Axumite farmers will stumble across another structure, palace, or remnant of the original mighty Axum Empire, yet no regular archeological digs are consistent there.

Today, in many cases, you don't have to look far to see the poverty and disease, but you also see right alongside the history and the growth. It's a truly odd mixture but one that has been the norm for centuries in Africa. Whenever I'm in Ethiopia for research and exploration, I am literally in tears over the suffering of these people. But, without any doubt, they have become survivors. They have a love and a care for each other like I have never seen before. They also reach out that hand to you. From the moment I stepped off the plane the first time and journeyed into this ancient land, while dodging camels and donkey carts, and watching as thousands shrouded in their robes walked through the dusty deserts, over the rocky mountain sides to do their daily routines, it didn't take long to realize that these people have a faith and a love lost in the materialized countries of this world.

The village of Axum, Ethiopia is without a doubt one of the most mystifying places on Earth. In this highland, desert location, it houses some of history's greatest treasures. Unlike the well-preserved artifacts and historical sites that we encounter in the United States, in Ethiopia they are, in many cases, recognized but still unprotected and withering away. When you arrive in Axum in many locations, you quickly feel like you dropped back in time 2,000 years. Other than small taxies and work trucks, the inhabitants of this ancient land walk, ride on donkey-pulled carts, or by camel. Dusty, rocky roads and open markets are the common place. White robed adorned people are the majority, and the buildings and structures stand in an apparent time warp alongside new hotels and condominiums. There is a real biblical-like feeling to this ancient place that totally defies description.

However, this remotely nestled Ethiopian town does make a most dramatic assertion to its credit. Axum is the only place in the world that claims to house the Holy Ark of the Covenant in a daubed chapel, Saint Mary of Zion Church, which has been its resting place for centuries. The building is surrounded by a high pointed iron fence and is heavily guarded. The interesting thing about Axum is that they don't publicize the fact that they have the Ark, and they really don't care if you come to their city or not, as a visitor or tourist. They simply claim that God has allowed them to be the guardians of the Ark until the time comes for the calling of its return to Israel.

The Guardian of the Ark, chosen for his purity and believed to be of the line to the Levites, gives his life to stay within the fenced-in area of the church and guard the Ark until he dies. Once chosen this man will never leave the grounds of this church again and agrees to completely remove himself from his family and friends. Even though it's an honor to be chosen as the Guardian, it is also somewhat sad to see his apparent loneliness. But that is from a westerner's point of view. The honor that he holds as the only human allowed to view the Ark of the Covenant may outweigh that he has given up everything in life to serve God in this way. When you truly grasp the situation from that point of view, maybe that's the ultimate responsibility of worship in the first place, to give up everything we have in life to serve God, as Christ asked us to do in the Scriptures.

The Guardian at some point, chooses a young boy who, matching the same qualifications, enters the gates of the complex to be trained as the new Guardian. The boy, once he crosses the gate, will never be able to leave the complex again, realizing the honor that he has been given. That boy will be given the honor to learn the ceremonial ways of the position and to eventually take the position of his teacher. Shortly after our first arrival in Axum, our team was given a rare opportunity for the Guardian to meet us at the back gate. This was the first time to see him up-close, rather than seeing him from a distance walking around the courtyard of the church of the Ark. Quietly he approached us at a back-gate. While they never opened the gate, he reached through the iron fence to provide a blessing upon our team. This wouldn't be the last time I would encounter this man in this journey, but it was the first and one that I will always remember.

In one particular corner of Axum, you will see a collection of massive towering stelae (obelisks) to commemorate each of the mighty kings or successful battles of the Axumite Empire. On this site, you will also find the underground tombs of the great kings of the Axumite Empire. During the occupation of Mussolini in 1937 during World War II in Ethiopia, the dictator wanted to claim the Ark of the Covenant. The story has it that when the Ark was lowered and whisked away into the hundreds of miles of underground tunnels under the church of the Ark, that Mussolini, in his anger, dismantled the second largest of the stelae, and took it away on trucks to the Red Sea, and shipped it away. For many years, it stood at the Piazza di Porta Capenemin in Rome, near the Arch of Constantine. In 2005, the 160-ton obelisk was finally returned to its rightful place in Axum, where they have taken great care to re-erect the structure in its original resting place.

A few hundred yards away is the legendary bathing pool of the Queen of Sheba. Even though the water is extremely dirty and contaminated with disease, it has become a constant water supply, a place to wash clothes, and to bathe. It also serves as a key spiritual site for the second day of the ceremony of Timkat, recognizing the baptism of Christ. Next to the bathing pool is a rocky road that moves up the mountain to the excavated palace remains and tombs of other great kings such as the mighty King Kaleb and King Gebre Meskel. Just a few yards past their tombs is a breathtaking view of the Adwa Mountain range. Near the great stelae are other tombs, including the powerful King Ezana, who is credited with bringing the Christian faith to Ethiopia.

In their possession, they also claim to have many artifacts that came from Solomon's temple, along with the Ark of the Covenant. If this were true, I knew that I had to see it for myself. We were given special permission to go into the treasury located next the church of the Ark, a former underground bunker. Within their treasury of the Ark, they house the solid gold crowns of the kings, the robes that adorned these rulers, their reigning staffs, along with many artifacts sharing the history of this proud country during their many great years of power and favorability.

While I stood in front of a wooden dusty shelf, looking at the crowns, the rest of the group went farther into the building to view the reported covering that was over the Ark when it arrived in Axum; I started to sweat profusely. My hands began to tingle and numb, and I started to feel somewhat sick. Since I was alone, I felt I needed to brace myself, so I reached forward to the shelf that contained ancient solid gold crowns of kings, many of which have diamonds, rubies, and emeralds attached throughout. This instantly attracted the attention of the treasury armed guard. I then twisted backwards, dropping to the floor and onto my knees. This was a point that the past became the present. It was then that I saw them. It took me back to Gatlinburg when the woman put the necklace around my neck, where it still rested. Everyone else had passed these by.

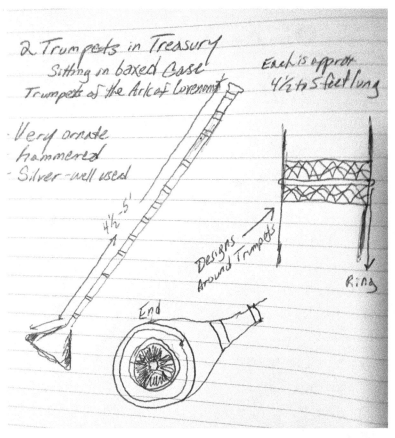

2 Trumpets in Treasury
Sitting in boxed Case
Trumpets of the Ark of Covenant ⟶

Each is approx.
4½ to 5 feet long

· Very ornate
· hammered
· Silver - well used

5'
4½

Designs
Around Trumpets

Ring

End

Jim's original sketch inside the treasury of the ancient hammered silver
trumpets of the Ark

Before me were what appeared to be two large silver trumpets, each nearly five feet in length. Since the guard was already
on his way, so was the treasury curator and Misgana, my trusted
friend and guide. I asked Misgana what these trumpets were.
Through Misgana's translation, the curator said, "These are the
trumpets of Moses from what is said to be from Bible's book
of Numbers. These trumpets came to Axum with the Ark of the
Covenant from Solomon's temple. These are the hammered

silver trumpets of Moses." Even though the numbing stopped, the sweating began to increase as I started to think, "Am I kneeling in front of the two actual trumpets that Moses had in his hand? Am I really looking at these, while the Holy Ark is just fifty yards from me in the building next door?" As he spoke I reached to the trumpets necklace around my neck, as tears began to flow. It was obvious that these trumpets were ancient pounded silver. Each of them had rings around them to possibly signify the twelve tribes of Israel. I asked if I could hold one. The curator understood and simply smiled, shook his head, and said, "No, no." I quickly grabbed my wife who shared my emotion, and she began to tear up as well. This became a theme to our team shortly after leaving the building. "When the trumpets call, arise and go?" This awareness escalated my excitement, and my anticipation of future adventure gave me an adrenaline rush that will never leave. To this day, I have not lost the passion for this adventure, this calling of the trumpets of Moses.

Why would God choose such a place to house the Ark of the Covenant, and His throne, the Mercy Seat? It's a place riddled with poverty and illness, yet abounding in love. It's a place that time has forgotten, yet one of the most amazing visions I have ever seen. It's not a typical vacation site, but in its own way it's a place of beauty, not only for its landscape of desert mountain views, beautiful eagles and hawks soaring through the skies, and ancient artifacts and sites, but because of the people that inhabit this land. These are a people who have been trodden down and forgotten, but carry a proud and unselfish beauty with them through their lives. Maybe this would be the perfect place to hide the Ark, until the time that it will be called upon again.

THE MYSTERIOUS LALIBELA, ETHIOPIA

Stone Church of St. George in Lalibela, Ethiopia. Notice its cross shape, standing over three stories tall.

To the south of Axum and high into the mountains, we then make our way to Lalibela. This mountain-top village is one of the most incredible places on this earth. Nowhere else will you be able to see the amazing sites found in this ancient village in the upper mountainous regions of Ethiopia. History has it that the rightful heir to the throne at Roha (the modern-day Lalibela) was a young boy named Gebre Mesqel Lalibela. At birth, a swarm of bees surrounded him, and his mother named him Lalibela, which means "bees recognize his sovereignty." This also was a sign to his mother that he would one day become the emperor of Ethiopia. Lalibela was in conflict with his uncle, Tatadim, and his own brother, King Kedus Harbe. He was also nearly poisoned to death by a half-sister during this inner family battle. During this time, Lalibela went into exile in Jerusalem for several years.

During his time in Israel, he gained great knowledge, and felt that he was given a vision to bring the Holy Land back to his home and retake his rightful throne. This could have been because during this time period Israel had been invaded and was in much disarray and destruction. Many historians believe that since Lalibela's brother was still alive when he returned to his homeland, that he took the throne by force. So, the self-proclaimed rightful heir to the throne was now the King of Ethiopia, and began to transfer Roha into a New Jerusalem. He brought with him olive trees from Israel and renamed the hillside the Mount of Olives. He also changed the name of the small river that flows through the town to be called the River Jordan.

Considering that the entire city is on top of a mountain of a reddish–pink granite, this is what makes Roha (later named Lalibela to honor their king) different from any other place on earth. In this mountain top, poverty driven community, you will find the most amazing carvings ever created. Somehow, King Lalibela in just over two decades, carved eleven rock-hewn churches down into the top of the mountain. One of them is the famous Church of St. George, or Bete Giyorgis, which is shaped like an Ethiopian cross, and can only be entered by following a tunnel and choosing the right direction of a cave to pass through. Then after making the correct decision, you will finally come out to the open area of the church. Many believe that this church was constructed to house the Ark of the Covenant, which never arrived there.

The largest of these structures is the Bet Medhane Alem church, which was reported to be the home of the Lalibela cross. In recent returns to Lalibela, and more precisely this church, I have been given the honor to hold the solid gold cross of Lalibela in my hands. It is also said to be the largest monolithic church in the world with its massive pillars and many rooms within. Next door is the Church of St. Mary, which lays claim to have the secrets of how these churches were constructed in such a short period of time. Lalibela claimed this was accomplished with the help of angels, while others around the world claim different theories. The secret to their construction is said to be beyond a tall pillar inside the church, in the area known as the Holy of Holies. This section is heavily guarded, and no one is allowed beyond the shrouded pillar to investigate. This particular church is also believed to have a model, or copy, of the original church of the Ark, Saint Mary of Zion Church, in Axum. Another one of the amazing churches worth mentioning is Bete Golgotha, which is believed to be the final resting place of King Lalibela. I have been given opportunity in this place, and I believe there is much more to this mysterious location of the king's tomb, but that's for another journey at another time. No matter who built them and how they did it, the churches of Lalibela are an important and credible wonder of this world.

The journey to Lalibela is not an easy one, but one that was well worth trekking around the world to see. This city is one of the holiest places in Ethiopia, second only to Axum because of its belief to be the home of the Ark of the Covenant. This amazing place left me awe struck as I stood on the mountainside next to ancient olive trees, and looked around at beautiful reddish-pink granite monuments that in many ways lay in tribute to a former king and his inspired vision to recreate the Holy Land in his home town, but also to be a front of protection to even more secrets held within their walls. Regardless of who helped this king carve out these beautiful and mesmerizing structures, one look at their sharp edges and near perfect construction will show that God's hand had to be in this masterpiece. The churches were so perfectly made that each one has been constructed with a natural water flow underneath the rock to keep the wells filled with water. How did Lalibela do it? That's a question that still baffles the architects, the engineers, and the world, centuries after their construction. The mystery will continue, but the truth will be revealed when it is time. (*ref. 12*).

THE CAMELOT OF GONDAR, ETHIOPIA

The castle of King Fasilides in Gondar, Ethiopia. Note the shape of the Lion of Judah, the head to the upper right, four towers are the legs, and the wall goes around the courtyard like the tail.

This is truly an interesting place, known as the Camelot of Ethiopia, and a place of many hidden secrets. Gondar was founded by Emperor Fasilides around 1635, and it feels, in many ways, like you're in the middle of a medieval novel. The claim to Camelot comes from their many castles built by former Emperors who reigned there. This became the capital city in Ethiopia, and Fasilides built his palace there along with seven churches scattered throughout the city. No one really knows why Fasilides chose Gondar to build his empire, but the tradition has been given of a story that included a buffalo that led the king to a pool where a hermit proclaimed to him that he would build his kingdom there. The pool was filled, and his castle was built on that spot *(ref 13)*. In reality there was, and is, a constant spring that was originally located on that spot, and it is reported that it is still there today where a cistern receives its water from. There is also a claim that goes well beyond the time of Fasilides, and farther back into biblical accounts of an event that took place at this site. This was known by many and gives more reason to why the king would have constructed his castle on this spot. But that's another adventure to be investigated in future times. Regardless, King Fasilides' claim to this place brought life to not only the city but also the region that surrounds it. Five emperors who followed him also built their palaces there. One factor to understand about most of the kings that proceeded this time period was that many dwelled in temporary royal encampments and had no permanent palaces. There are exceptions to this rule, however, with the powerful empires that have since been uncovered in areas such as the Axumite Kingdom and others.

During a visit to Gondar, located north of Lake Tana, you will notice a distinct difference in this city. You will be quick to notice the castles all throughout the area, along with a great deal of Italian influence because of the Italian occupation during their conquest in 1936 and again as Italy's last stand in World War II against the English. You can still see ruins from the wars, including one particular site that houses Mussolini's bunker atop one of the mountains.

The incredible castles and palaces are show-stoppers in this ancient city. It has been the basis for many battles, and traditionally it was divided into quarters for its diversity of residents. One of those residents includes Beta Israel, or more commonly known at the Falashian Jews. Although thousands of these Ethiopian Jews were air-lifted to Jerusalem during a series of evacuations in the 1990's, this is the site in which their origin was based, dating back to the time of Moses, with ties to the Queen of Sheba's son, Menelik. The Jews in this region are heavily persecuted and many have been killed for their claims and beliefs. It's believed that because of their direct lines to possibly either the tribes of Dan or Benjamin, they may be the ones responsible for the returning of the Ark of the Covenant to Jerusalem upon Christ's return. It is also claimed that there are still remnants of the Tribe of Levi existing here.

Gondar is a place that provides magnificent views of the rough African terrain while standing atop the mountains that surround it. Even though poverty and disease are seen throughout this location, as it is in all of Ethiopia, Gondar is truly a gem resting among the stony landscape. The castles offer up glorious days of knights riding into the kingdom while a sense of intrigue fills the air about some of the darker days that were sure to have passed in and out of the ages of time during the reigns of various emperors. But you will also see much growth including universities, hospitals, and other opportunities becoming more visible in this area.

The "Church of the Bees" or Debra Berhan Selassie Church in Gondar, Ethiopia may hold many other hidden secrets.

One of the show-stoppers in Gondar is the Debra Berhan Selassie Church which is more commonly known as The Light of the Trinity Church. It was built by Emperor Eyasu II in the 17th century, and today is one of Ethiopia's most important churches. During a battle in 1888, the Mahdist Dervishes of the Sudan ransacked the city and burned down every church in the city with the exception of Debra Berhan Selassie. Legend has it that when the forces approached the church, a swarm of bees flew down surrounding the church, and thwarted the attempt to destroy the structure. It is also believed by the Ethiopians that during this swarming of the bees, the Archangel Michael stood with a flaming sword, as if to guard the wooden gates leading to the church *(ref. 14)*. Either way, it still holds to an exciting story of the existence of this stone-walled and thatched roofed church, with some of the country's most beautiful painted walls and ceilings depicting many biblical scenes, the Trinity, and hundreds of angels covering from top to bottom. It also may hold other secrets as well. It may be a historic marker to other events that once took place nearby this ancient city that relates more to the real reason Fasilides chose the site for his castle.

Although the poverty can be seen at every turn, Gondar was still uniquely compelling for us during our travels. As a matter of fact, our guide, Misgana, purchased a large portion of property atop one the highest mountains in Gondar where he built a beautiful resort in order to attract visitors to the beauty and sites of the Camelot of Ethiopia.

TO THE SHORES OF BAHIR-DAR

Ancient monastery located on one of Lake Tana's islands.

Barhir Dar, located on the southern banks of the mighty Lake Tana in Ethiopia, is unique for many reasons. It is a popular tourist spot because of Lake Tana, which is the start of the Blue Nile River and the beautiful Blue Nile Falls. Barhir Dar is known for their palm-lined streets and friendly people. It has a heavy Ethiopian Orthodox religion base, while at the same time, a growing population of Muslims inhabit the city, which adds a different perspective than most other locations in Ethiopia. Despite the high volume of the Orthodox faith in Ethiopia, there still exists a looming concern throughout this region over the last several years because of the strong Muslim growth. Although according to the Quran (Book of Battles), the Prophet Muhammad called for Ethiopia to be protected from war against them, because of a return gesture of generosity by an Axumite king during the first migration spoken of in the book.

This is a beautiful city to all standards in Ethiopia. Palm trees can be seen throughout, as well as Jacaranda trees which add a colorful touch when in full bloom. The Blue Nile Falls remains one of Ethiopia's biggest attractions, and it draws thousands to this region each year. This natural wonder bursts out of Lake Tana with a drenching mist, bringing truth to the name of the "water that smokes." It's a lush tropical setting, with an occasional rainbow splashing color into the mist. Lake Tana is another desirable site in this region of Ethiopia, as it is nestled in the mountainous area of the country. When flying to this massive lake, you will notice the arrival well before you even see the lake, because of the lush countryside of green that beckons you.

Lake Tana is Ethiopia's largest lake, dawning plentiful wildlife, and it's the starting point to one of the most famous rivers in the world, the great Nile River, which runs northward through Egypt. The Blue Nile River, which later meets with the White Nile to form the Nile River is home to nearly three dozen islands, including Tana Kirkos, Daga Stephanos, and the Zege Pennisula. These islands contain many monasteries with monks and priests giving the appearance to be somewhat guardians of the islands. Some of the islands contain lost scrolls, tombs of emperors, and ancient palace or temple remains.

Barhir Dar is the primary city docking against the lake, and gained its popularity and growth from the masses that come to take in the beauty of this pristine body of water. But Barhir Dar held other purposes preceding World War II. After the Italians took over Gondar in 1937, they moved south to Barhir Dar. The English Royal Air Force bombed Barhir Dar in 1940 causing the Italians to retreat back to Gondar. One interesting note is that throughout Ethiopia, ruins of destroyed buildings and vehicles can be seen dating back to their many conflicts, but also because of the remnants of the Second World War *(ref.15)*. Today in Barhir Dar you may have to look a little harder because of the recent tourist market in the city has encouraged the dismanteling of these past conflicts.

With its constant growth, this city continues to be one of the most visited in Ethiopia. Then, of course, it is believed that at one point in time, around 410 BC, the Ark of the Covenant would have moved through this area, before the founding of the city, and rested well off the shores of the lake on Tana Kirkos Island. Emperor Selassie's (Ethiopian's King from 1930-1974) palace is located near Barhir Dar and he was responsible for building one of the large highway bridges over the Abay. Even though this city is unique and beautiful, it is one of the most important to the early foundations of Ethiopian prominence in the Bible.

A FINAL LOOK

These are just a few of the sites of the northern mountain regions of Ethiopia, but probably the most common to the holy nature of the country. So much turmoil has taken place in this region over the centuries. Both civil wars and world battles have used Ethiopia as a ground of conflict throughout the ages. Great wealth turned to great poverty since the times of the early kings of this biblical nation. But one thing is for sure, the northern region of Ethiopia has been a hot spot of spiritual quests throughout the centuries. This truly could be the location of many of the God's mysterious secrets, from the housing of His throne, to an incredible meeting with His Son. It is an overwhelming feeling that this could be the place where we will hear those trumpets blast again, and the world will see a sign from these mountains that will be heard and seen from around the globe.

Chapter 5:

LOOKING OVER THE MYSTERIOUS LAKE

SOMEHOW, I KNEW AS I was standing on the cliff over-looking the village of Axum on our final night before embarking on the next leg of our journey, that our adventure had really only begun. As the sun was setting with a bronze finish spreading over the land, I reviewed the last few days in my mind and referred back to my journal. It was at this point that it really started to press upon me. We had explored the tombs of ancient kings, in a rare opportunity met with the Guardian of the Ark, fell to my knees before the incredible hammered silver trumpets that the treasury curator claims to be those of Moses, took part in the Timkat ceremony, and experienced a spiritual rush when we shared the Gospel to wonderful young man. Through all of this remembrance, I couldn't help but think that something else was still to come. By this time, the sun had dipped behind the mountains and a chill had come over this land. I slipped on my jacket, and was joined by Dave Kochis on the terrace. He soon saw the thought process that was obviously written on my face. He said, "It's really wonderful here, isn't it?" "It all is!" I replied. "But, Dave do you ever feel like God took you somewhere to remove you from everything you are comfortable with, just so He can shut you down long enough to show you something really big?" Dave exclaimed, "Yes, and I think that is why we are both here, but for different reasons. I feel God is helping me from a personal standpoint, and I think He's got something else in store for you." That left me in even more wonder. Sherri came out to join us, and she quickly saw in my eyes that I had been in deep thought. She is always quick to see these things in me, and can always read me whether I'm hurting, worried, fearful, angry or happy. Arm in arm, we told Dave goodnight, and made our way down the dark concrete steps, past an old sycamore tree, to our room for the night. Laying there with my eyes staring at the ceiling, I couldn't wait to see what was next. I spent many nights in Ethiopia looking up at the ceiling. The information overload could only be processed in the darkness and silence before retiring each night.

Morning arrived, and we loaded up our van and worked our way down the mountain, back through Axum, to the one runway airport located on the outskirts of this ancient village. Before we pulled into the airport, we couldn't help but notice the remnants of an old military bunker that was more than likely from the Italian battle against English in World War II, or from one of their many civil wars. As we turned to our final roadway to the airport, a young armed guard dressed in blue camouflage stopped us, and ordered us out of our van. He wanted passports to confirm our identities. Even though toting a machine gun, and trying to give stern instructions, the soldier was more than willing to take a photo opportunity to display his gun with our group. I believe this example proves the love of these people, and their passion for peace in their hearts.

MARY ON THE MOUNTAIN

We boarded a turbo prop plane and started on our journey to Gondar, located north of Lake Tana. It was a short flight, and as we cleared the clouds we were immediately on the runway, whisking side to side in frantic stop before running off the end of the pavement. A man on a camel rode by waving as we exited the plane, and walked across the tarmac to the building. Misgana's men were there waiting for us and loaded our bags as we hopped on another van and made our way to Gondar. We had arrived in the Camelot of Ethiopia, and much of its ancient roots were riveted in the history of the medieval castles still standing tall today. Our purpose for visiting Gondar was not to take in the architecture, but to head to the top of one of the mountains in search of a woman and her village, which is claimed to be one of the most ancient areas of the remaining Falasha Jews.

As we scurried up the rocky dirt road, I noticed a series of very large, four to five-foot tall mud statues of the Lion of Judah with a Star of David on their heads. It was like each little hut had one in their front. Bob Cornuke jokingly said, "The first person to point out Mary (the Falashian woman we were searching for) wins a prize." I stepped out of the van and a feeling overwhelmed me, as I turned left and said, "There she is, Bob." He stared at me as if to say, "How did he know that?" Although I can't answer that one, I knew this was the woman we had come to see. We learned of her family being killed trying to return to her from Israel, and many Falashians on that mountain had been killed, or disappeared, for their beliefs.

Pictured left to right: Sherri, Mary, Jim.

We sat in a make-shift hut as Mary, through Misgana translating, shared her sad story as tears rolled down her face. Larry, one of the men on the expedition with us, took a cloth and reached over to wipe her tears. Seeing her pain while attempting to share the agony of her struggles, persecutions, and the loss of her family was beyond belief and almost made us all forget why we had come. But now it was time to continue what we came to do. Kathryn Pierce, a nurse who had been a part of the exploration team, pulled out swabs to get an inside cheek sample for a DNA test to be done back in the states. It was all to determine if Mary was truly one of the Falashian Jews or possibly a direct line to the legendary Levite Jewish tribe. Mary was timid at first, but allowed Kathryn to continue with the swabbing. Just when I thought it was time to go, my wife and I turned back. In her small hut home were Sherri, Misgana, Mary and me. I looked at Mary as I asked Misgana to tell her it was a privilege to be in her home. Misgana introduced me as a holy man from America, and what happened next was nothing less than a miracle. The woman who only could speak in the ancient Amharic language leaned over, grabbed my shoulders, and said to me, "I know Jesus." Dazed and confused, my wife and I stepped back and looked at each other, as if to say, "Did you hear that?" But, what was really confusing is that our guide, Misgana, never flinched; he heard nothing. Sherri, still filming, stood with her mouth open and tears streaming down her face. Mary's tears were non-stop, and at this point I really didn't know what to do next. We turned and headed to the opening of her hut and made our way outside. In front of her home was a large stone fire stove, which was also used as a kiln for firing her pottery. I noticed this as we entered and that it had recently been used. Mary had a little wood handmade shelf sitting right outside her door with small terracotta pots and miniature Lions of Judah with the Star of David on their heads, matching the much larger ones lining the dirt road coming up the mountain. With Sherri still filming, Mary reached over and grabbed one of her coffee pots, looked for my wife, and handed the pot to her as a gift. Nearly dropping the camera, she hugged Mary, again in tears. She then turned to me and handed me a Lion of Judah. It was an incredible feeling to know we may have just witnessed God speaking through this woman. This was a woman who had such a visible sadness about her, but a calmness to her demeanor that you just don't see unless someone is filled with peace. Later study of our video footage would show that Mary spoke in her native tongue on the video, but when it came to our ears it was plainly in English. It was an incredible blessing to be with Mary, and one that will always stay with me for the rest of my life. Today, Mary has become a great friend to us all. She has a picture of Sherri and me hanging on her wall, which is a great honor for us.

Following our visit with Mary, we headed across the mountain to the highest point of the immediate range to where Misgana had purchased land in order to build a beautiful resort upon. As a boy, Misgana had been taken away from the island where he was raised on Lake Tana, beaten, and forced to serve as a child soldier. To look at him now, a successful Ethiopian guide, travel company owner, and hotel designer, it can only make you have hope for anyone in any dire situation to succeed. Misgana has never given up from his early struggles and is now on the journey of his life-long dream. He has hopes of even more resorts in Bahir Dar, Axum, and other areas as well. As for his Gondar location, one quick glance and you will see that something was different about the mountain top that he had given his life savings to develop. All around are the remains of military bunkers on his property. Misgana pointed out to us some of the features of his resort, when I asked him what one particular, blown-apart remains of a building was, he explained that in World War II it was the bunker of Benito Mussolini, or what was left of it. This was the highest mountain point in the area, and the Italians used it as a stronghold in their final battles against the English. By the looks of it, Mussolini's bunker didn't fare very well in their final battles. I think the English may have gotten the best of this particular bunker. The view was beautiful, and it didn't take us long to see the excitement of Misgana for his investment and his future vision.

TRAVELING TO BAHIR DAR

After our descent down the mountain, we began the long journey to the south. As we traveled through the skyscraper mountain tops, the storybook African huts could be seen all around. At one point, we had a desert on the left and a jungle with monkeys screaming on the right. One thing we found very quickly, you better have a good ear, because if you don't hear the horn of the rare oncoming vehicle you would quickly become road-kill. The sight of a passing van or truck are few; the most common view is people by the hundreds walking the roads and streets to and from their destination. Some are simply walking, while others are guiding their herds, traveling on camel, or on donkey carts carrying massive loads of goods on their shoulders, heads and backs. Many times, especially when passing through the villages, the driver would beep the horn, never leaving his path or slowing down, and if you were ever in the way, Lord help you! They do not stop for anyone or anything. I asked the driver at one point if he had ever hit anyone and his reply nonchalant was, in his Amharic accent, "Many." That was a little scary. I encourage you to keep this in mind if ever walking along the road in Africa! If you hear a horn, move quickly, or you might become another notch on the belt of the wild drivers of Ethiopia.

A massive stone tower called the "finger of God" by the Ethiopians, hundreds of feet tall.

As we traveled, we came to a massive stone tower powering out of the hillside like a New York City skyscraper, and straight up several hundreds of feet. One of our translators said it was called the "finger of God." This was in the area where the mountains protruded high and the lushness of the landscape greened up under it. The "finger of God" looked like a high-rise building exploding from the trees and peeking into the Ethiopian skyline. It was near Lake Tana as we could see the sparkling of the water at certain points glistening on the other side of the mountains. It was so picturesque that it appeared to be an illusion. We made a stop at the "finger of God" for a bathroom break. I escorted Sherri about a hundred yards off the roadway to a large rock and stood watch for her. Then, rather than standing watch for me, she wandered back to the roadway, and left me standing alone behind the rock. As I stood there, out of nowhere, from the desert in front of me, a boy appeared and waved to me as he walked by. I don't know where he came from, but the encounter didn't faze him like it startled me. When I returned to the group, I saw people swarming everywhere. It was like people were moving rocks and crawling up out of the ground. I don't know from where, but our vans were surrounded by children hoping for a sticker or piece of candy. There was not a hut or house to be seen for miles, but from the hillsides these kids appeared. It was an awesome sight, and this precious memory still lingers with me. As we continued traveling, I started noticing caves in the mountain sides and realized that these kids probably called those indentions in rock home.

Finally, after half a day's drive we arrived in Barhir Dar, which rests on the southern bank of Lake Tana, Ethiopia's largest lakes. Without a doubt, it is a rather unusual town. Each morning you will hear the chanting of prayers, almost rivaling each other, broadcasting over loud speakers from both the Orthodox churches and the Muslims. The people are gracious, but with a very different feel than that of Axum. After arriving at our motel, Sherri and I followed our adventurous nature to check out the area, and we headed out to the bustling town square. As the taxis frantically hovered around the circle square, it reminded me of a life-size version of the old video game Frogger. It was hit or miss, just to get from one side of the street to the other. Although many that we came in contact with carried the Ethiopian kindness that we had grown familiar with in other areas, it was not the majority in Barhir Dar. We were definitely an outsider, and we could feel it.

BIBLE STUDY FOLLOWING THE ARK TO ETHIOPIA

After returning to the motel, our research team gathered under the canopy near the lobby for a Bible study. It was during this time that a reality began to set in. It was a reality that I began to understand that this mission wasn't necessarily about the Ark of the Covenant, but much more than that. Just like Dave had said to me on the cliff-side in Axum, we each had something God was trying to open up to us. He said that his was a personal reason for being on this expedition, and my reason was going to be a little different. As Bob laid out the Scripture from the Bible to the reference of why the Ark could very well be in Axum, and how it spent some time near Barhir Dar, it started to press on my mind and heart that all I had seen thus far was a pathway of bread crumbs leading me to this mysterious lake. It was a continuing thought, similar to a skipping record on an old scratchy record player, which kept jumping back to each step of this journey, leading right up to this night. Then it would all start again. I knew that the next day would bring a revelation that none of us were expecting. It was like the night couldn't end soon enough to get on with the adventure still to come. Bob went through the evidence on the theory on the Ark of the Covenant being housed in Ethiopia as a holding place for its return to Jesus. He shared that according to Scriptures, it was definite that at the time of Hezekiah, the Ark remained in Jerusalem at that time:

> *And Hezekiah prayed before the LORD, and said, O LORD God of Israel, which dwellest between the cherubims, thou art the God.* (2 Kings 19:15)

Then, more than likely it disappeared around the time of the reign of the evil King Manasseh, Hezekiah's son, who defiled the temple and brought disgrace to Israel:

> *And he did that which was evil in the sight of the LORD, after the abominations of the heathen, whom the LORD cast out before the children*

of Israel. For he built up again the high places
which Hezekiah his father had destroyed; and
he reared up altars for Baal...and worshipped
all the host of heaven, and served them. And
he built altars in the house of the LORD, of
which the LORD said, In Jerusalem will I put
my name. And he built altars for all the host
of heaven in the two courts of the house of the
LORD. (2 Kings 21:2-7, 16)

Bob explained that at the same time, a temple modeled after Solomon's had been built on Elephantine Island, near Aswan, in Southern Egypt in the Nile River. Then, jumping past King Manasseh's son, Amon, to Josiah, who became king at a very young age, we see a prophecy opened up. Josiah made it an obsession to cleanse Israel from the evil of his grandfather and return it to its honor and standing with God. A great Passover feast took place during this time of cleansing and it was during this period that a great famine was cast over Israel. A telling Scripture is found in 2 Kings 23 where we learn that it was prophesized that God would bring Israel down because of Manasseh's evil, but not until after Josiah would be killed. Then something startling happens. The Scriptures show Josiah's demanding cry-out to the Levites to return the Ark to the temple of Solomon:

"Put the holy ark in the house which Solomon
the son of David king of Israel did build; it shall

*not be a burden upon your shoulders: serve now
the LORD your God, and his people Israel,"* (2
Chronicles 35:3)

We see that the Ark was not in Solomon's Temple and that
the Levites must have it in their possession, because they were
carrying it in proper fashion by the poles propped upon their
shoulders:

"they should bear upon their shoulders"
(Number 7:9)

But then things really get interesting. Since we now see that
the Ark was not in Jerusalem, we had to question, "Then, where
was it?" Bob went on to tell us that the last part of Josiah's plea
in 2 Chronicles 35:3 was for the Levites to begin serving God in
Israel once again. That tells us that the Ark of the Covenant was
no longer in Israel. This takes us back to Egypt and Elephantine
Island. Ancient writings found at the site show that the priests
referenced as God "dwelling there," or in the "presence of
the Lord," which is a direct comparison to Scripture phrasing
the same fact when discussing God's presence was with the
Ark. But the best biblical evidence that the Ark was in Egypt
was during the confrontation of King Josiah and the Egyptian
Pharaoh Necho:

*"After all this, when Josiah had prepared the
temple, Necho king of Egypt came up to fight*

> *against Carchemish by Euphrates: and Josiah*
> *went out against him."* (2nd Chronicles 35:20)

Josiah, in his efforts to have God's presence return to the Israel, seemed to be blinded by his obsession to return the Ark to the temple. His obsession moved him to attempt to battle against the mighty army of Egypt in an unnecessary war, considering that Necho was out to battle the Babylonians. So Necho, in his passing by, and trying to keep peace, sends out messengers to Josiah:

> *"But he sent ambassadors to him, saying, What*
> *have I to do with thee, thou king of Judah? I come*
> *not against thee this day, but against the house*
> *wherewith I have war:"* (2 Chronicles 35:21a)

But the biggest and most shocking statement delivered by Necho was:

> *"for God commanded me to make haste:"* (2 Chronicles 35:21b)

Stone carving of Egyptian Pharaoh Necho.

We learn two very startling facts with that explanation from the Egyptian Pharaoh. First, the Egyptian king was telling Josiah that Jehovah God was giving him the orders. You see, this leader didn't follow tradition, and he wasn't serving the gods of Egypt's past. He was actually getting his commands directly from the One God. Then, in closing, Necho scolds Josiah with this statement:

> *"forbear thee from meddling with God, who is with me, that he destroy thee not."* (2nd Chronicles 35:21)

Necho tells Josiah to back away because God was literally with him on this quest. In other words, Necho knew God Almighty, and Josiah would be wise to stay out of their business. But Scripture tells us that the warning from Necho was not enough:

> *"Nevertheless Josiah would not turn his face from him, but disguised himself, that he might fight with him, and hearkened not unto the words of Necho from the mouth of God"* (2 Chronicles 35:22)

The Scripture goes on to tell us, in verse 23, that Josiah, after masking himself, went out into battle in his chariot, and was killed in the confrontation. This then would fulfill the prophecy mentioned before.

TRAVELING TO LAKE TANA

So, what happened to the Ark? Where did it go? In approximately the third century, BC, the temple on Elephantine Island was destroyed, and the Levites simply disappeared along with the Ark. It was at this same time that monks on the forbidden island of Tana Kirkos on Lake Tana claim that the Jewish tribe brought the Ark there. In a makeshift tabernacle, the Ark rested on the high guarded cliffs of this island for hundreds of years. As we learned earlier, King Ezana became a Christian around 305 A.D. and proclaimed it to his kingdom. It was also around this time that the king and his soldiers traveled to Tana Kirkos Island and claimed the Ark of the Covenant, then transported it and the two silver trumpets of Moses to his kingdom in Axum, where it still rests in waiting today.

I couldn't keep my mind on the rest of the study that was being laid out for our team. I am thankful that I had my video camera placed up on the back of the benches and filmed the study for future reference. Bits and pieces would get embedded in my mind with the majority passing right by me. I began to flip through the Scriptures to look at Matthew chapter 2, and then to Numbers chapter 10, and then to Isaiah chapter 18. It was like a tornado of information between my ears that I had never had before. The knowledge of the Scriptures was coming to light in a way that I had really never processed in times past. It was like God was giving me everything I needed to prepare me, enlighten me, and lift me spiritually for the next day. Listen, I'm one that has to read things over and over again to get it. But all of a sudden it all started to click. Scripture after Scripture started to become clear to me. Even though my head was spinning, everything that I had read, absorbed, and thought about was meshing like a mystical mad house. But what became clearly evident was that it was all making sense. The path of the Ark and its arrival in Ethiopia, and the future calling, were all part of the layout of this incredible journey. But what was still to come? Why all of this speculation? I couldn't quite figure it out, so after the study I stopped my friend, Dave Kochis. Dave and I looked at the information; he was having the same spinning feeling to why he was on this adventure, although from an entirely different perspective. I gained a great deal of respect for Dave during this journey. He has a passion and a wonderful, sensible knowledge that was very relaxing to me. Sherri and I were very thankful that Dave was a part of this journey, and it turned into a friendship that continues today. I felt, which turned out to be the truth, that Dave was re-identifying himself through something personal during our time here. He didn't even know what to expect, but it all became clear to him as our journey was coming to a close. We were fortunate to gain many wonderful friendships during our journey to Africa. Dave was certainly one of those, as were Kathryn Pearce, Bev Regehr, Craig and Meredith Newmaker, and others. Everyone had a purpose for going, and many found that God had another reason for them later. As for Sherri and me, we knew there was still something to come, and I couldn't wait until the next morning to venture on this lake to find out why God had allowed me to travel to this mysterious place.

Chapter 6:

THE SHROUDED ISLAND

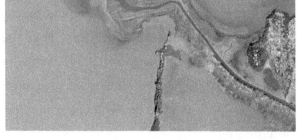

Top: Tana Kirkos Island arriving from the eastern side.
Bottom: Overhead view of Tana Kirkos Island. It's the narrow
strip in the center of the photo angling north to south.

MORNING HAD ARRIVED. FOR the last year and a half everything seemed to have been laid out without an ending. What was the ending? Why, at my age, had God opened up this incredible lifetime desire to search for the most sought-after artifact in history to me? Or, was that what it was all about anyhow? I had to believe there was more to come. Just as Sherri had said just four days prior to the call inviting us on this journey, "Jim, I really feel that our biggest and best adventures are still to come," I couldn't help but believe that something totally life-changing was going to happen. The dream in the middle of the night about the Ark connected for me with the invitation to be a part of this expedition for the truth about the Ark in Ethiopia. The perfect match with the two trumpets on the necklace that the lady in the shop in Gatlinburg, Tennessee handed me as a gift now came to light with the two hammered silver trumpets that were locked away in the hidden vault in Axum. That vault, of course, was next to the church that houses the once-thought lost Ark of the Covenant, that brought me to my knees. And even though during this journey, Sherri and I had developed a great passion for the people in this area of the world, we were also in agreement that our service to reach them through the New Testament gospel for Christ would be a long time future journey. We both also knew that something was still to come. Every aspect of the revelation to me in Tennessee had been put together like a big puzzle, with one giant piece in the middle still missing.

We started to look at this a little closer. What was still missing? The dream and two trumpets were complete. The theme of the journey had turned into "When the trumpets sound will you arise and go." This, of course, was in reference to an earlier devotion I gave to the group the night of the revealing of the trumpets in Axum. I shared the purpose of the trumpets to Moses as an instrument to call the people to the tabernacle because God had something to say. But then I jumped to Acts chapter 8 with the Ethiopian Eunuch and his encounter with Phillip. Prior to this meeting, God told Phillip to "Arise and go." Putting those two thoughts together, my devotion to the group was that each of us were called here, as if a trumpet sounded in our hearts. What the purpose was, may be an individual cleansing or revelation to each person. But I went on to say, when that trumpet sounds when we return home from this journey, will you take what you were given and arise and go, or follow-up on with what needs to be done? But, again, what was this piece that was missing in the puzzle? Or had I gone completely out of my mind? All I knew was that I needed to be patient and "Wait upon the Lord."

Morning had arrived, as we walked to the shoreline of the mighty Lake Tana, one glance across this massive mystical body of water appeared as though time had stood still with bulrush reed boats carrying fishermen in morning fog off in the distance. To the right, a variety of birds had congregated on the rocks to begin their morning fishing rituals, and the calming waters seemed to passively lay waiting as a lure to those who venture into the waters over the horizon. I was anxious but nervous as I boarded the small boat. As we cast off, the thought did occur whether this thing was even sea worthy. I overheard

Bob talking with Misgana about whether the waters were low enough for the captain to see the dangerous underwater rock formations. Misgana gave his typical answer, "No problem."

I started to review my notes about the missing link to this puzzle. The research team all loaded on and the boat's captain sounded the all clear as we turned from the dock and headed into a mysterious journey. Bob told us that the trip to the island of Tana Kirkos would take about three and half hours, one way. I couldn't help singing that song from the old television series, Gilligan's Island, about "A three-hour tour, a three-hour tour." Prayerfully, I hoped for safe passage and not the fate of those stranded in the comedy. The difference, this was a three-and-a-half-hour quest to an ancient and shrouded island full of mystery and guarded by monks.

At one point, Bev Regehr, Kathryn Pierce, Dave Kochis, along with a few others along with Sherri and I took part of the time to put together a strategy to reach the people for Christ on future return expeditions. After awhile, all had moved to shadier parts of the boat, as I pulled out my Bible and my notebook, and tried to figure out what piece of the puzzle was missing. It was one of those times where you think you should know the answer but it just wasn't clear. Then it was plain as day as the key to the missing piece came to me. It was the painting in Pigeon Forge, Tennessee that the lady had to show me, with Jesus and the Ark of the Covenant. If you remember from earlier, this painting was of the Ark plainly in the center with the Lion of Judah beside it, and then Jesus' face above it. The Lion of Judah was clearly laid out for me as we visited

Mary, the Falashian Jew, on the mountains around Gondar. The Lions of Judah were all through the village where Mary lived, made of mud with the Star of David upon their heads. I started to wonder about the Ark in the picture. Was that in reference to the Ark in Axum, or was something still to come? It was starting to clear up, but still the reference to Christ was still puzzling me. I tried to convince myself on a couple of wayward thoughts on this matter, but none took anchor. Then I worked in the idea, in convincing fashion, that Jesus in the painting was no more than a reference that Jesus was the keeper of the Commandments of God and became the Law. Unfortunately, my heart wasn't buying that.

THE ARK ON TANA KIRKOS ISLAND

Jim taking notes on the way to Tana Kirkos.

Eventually, after my hyperactively kicked in; I became anxious, and put away my Bible and notes, and sat my pack down secured on the deck of the boat. I walked around making conversation with members of the team while taking in the beauty of Lake Tana. I even proclaimed that if we had any problems with the hippos, we could throw Anita overboard as a sacrifice. This brought a laugh to the team as we pushed on across the lake. The calming waters were a pleasant foreground to the far distant shorelines and the passing islands. As we passed close enough to the islands, we would see large birds flapping from tree to tree, and monks kneeling by the waters fishing or washing their clothes. It was beautiful and actually calming to stare out into the distance.

After three and a half hours of belting sun, spraying water, and the buzzing of our boats engine, Misgana pointed ahead and told all of us that the island was just ahead. Far off in the distance the silhouette of an island could be seen. As we drew closer, it was noticeably different than most of the other islands we passed by. This island had towering cliffs at its base with papyrus surrounding it in the water. As we moved closer, a lone huge sycamore tree sat on a small piece of dry land at its base with something appearing to be jumping around in the tree. Then, way above all of the cliffs, towered another massive tree with two pristine oversized eagles sitting in its top, white heads and black bodies with awe inspiring wings stretched out in the sun. With my background with eagles, and Isaiah 40:31 as my favorite Scripture, I felt as though God had given me this as a sign that He was with me, and to follow along with what He was about ready to show me. Sherri saw it too, and turned and looked at me as though to say, "Here we go."

As the boat journeyed close to the island, the towering cliffs stretch over sixty feet above the waters, with what appeared to be a jungle on its top. The island was guarded by monks who choose boys from the mainland for their purity to be brought here to be trained. It has been this way for centuries. A group of monks had collected near the base of the island on huge rocks as though they were awaiting our arrival. One monk in particular was dressed in a long yellow robe, and a round head covering, and stood watching as the rest were ready to grab onto the boat. At first attempt the boat hit a series of rocks and the captain yelled out and reversed the engines. The Gilligan's Island theme started to run through my mind again. The captain made a simple move to the right and two of the monks yelled out this time as we plunged forward and hit rock again. One monk stepped down slightly into the water, realizing that these waters were infested with crocs and hippos, and waited for the boat to draw near as he guided it to a large rock, made like a makeshift dock.

Even though we tend to think and fear crocodiles, the truth is that the hippos take more lives in Africa than any other animal. Hippos can weigh up to three tons, and when they open their jaws they contain massive teeth with mouths big enough to grab a whole man. Even though hippos are vegetarians, they are very territorial and will attack anything that moves. Hippos even have been known in these waters to capsize large boats because they have crossed into their territory. Now, don't get me wrong, one glimpse at a twenty-two-foot crocodile and you'll realize that these are not waters to play around in. Whether it's a hippo, crocodile, or even a deadly snake, they are all forces of nature, and not to be tested.

Now that we were docked, two of the crew leaped from the boat with ropes and threw the ropes off to a couple of monks who tied them to a tree. Finally, three crashes in the rocks later, we were safely anchored to the forbidden island of Tana Kirkos. Bob stepped off of the boat to meet the man in yellow who happened to be the Aba, the head priest. After helping our party jump from the boat to the rocks, we all made our way up a broken-down opening in the cliffs to the top of the island. The rocks were dry, but very slick due to their use as the only way on and off the island for centuries. The island is about a mile long and probably only 100 yards across at its widest point. Other than the clearing at the top of the cliff where it seemed to be a mud-daubed building that the monks congregated in, the rest of the island appeared to be dense jungle. The Aba told Misgana that the women could go no further with us, but they would go with the monks to a church at the other end of the island, about a half mile to the north. As for us, we followed the Aba through the jungle. We followed a distinct trail, and at one point I saw what appeared to be a monkey jump across the trees above me. The walk was strenuous as we trekked along the high cliffs above the waters below. The temperatures were soaring, and the humidity was drenching as we pressed on through the jungle. I think at this point I would have been willing to move onward in any condition. I was on a mission of unspecified instruction and wasn't about to stop now.

ON HOLY GROUND

A Monk leading through the lush jungle pathway on Tana Kirkos Island.

As we walked through the lush jungle-like pathway, I had started to notice that I was sweating extremely heavily, and my arms had begun to tingle like they were falling asleep. We arrived at a small clearing in the trees and the feeling of numbness started into my arms, which was similar to the same feeling I had three days earlier in Axum when I fell in front of the trumpets. I began to think that the walk had gotten to me, and the heat had set in. On our left was an ancient stone building just large enough to have two levels. It was backed against the jungle and faced a twenty-five-foot cliff. A bulrush reed boat sat in front of the building on a set of rocks, and a monk rested in the shade by the door. I had the sneaking suspicion that someone else was watching us, as well. I looked around without seeing anyone. It was just a creepy feeling that other eyes were on us. Then I saw a monk in the trees behind the building peeking at us. I turned and looked and saw the face of another monk, as if they were keeping an eye on us to guard whatever was nearby. To my right was a stone archway with a rock fence, and through it was a larger stone and mud-daubed building with large stone and wood pillars, which was the holy temple of the monks. One of them said they called it the church of the Holy Ark. You could clearly hear the eerie sounds of a simple beat of a kebero drum in the building that had no doors, only shrouds hanging down. Along with the drums were chanting that came from the building as many of the monks were inside in prayer. I wondered if this was the same setting when the Ark of the Covenant rested somewhere near this place. I started to walk through the archway and Misgana stopped me

by grabbing my collar and said, "We have to remove our shoes."
He followed up, "You have to remove your shoes because now
you will walk on Holy ground." Within an instant I started to
sweat even more profusely as my mind flashed back to the
Scriptures:

> *"...put off thy shoes from off thy feet, for the*
> *place whereon thou standest is holy ground."*
> (Exodus 3:5)

It was as though I had heard this in a dream, or someone
else said this to me in preparation for our journey. Either way,
it was extremely eerie to hear those words. I put my hand up
against the archway and removed my hiking shoes. After we
stepped through, Bob pointed at a unique cross carved into the
wall of the cliff. He had us bring a shovel on the boat, which
one of our team carried for this purpose. He told us that the
cross was some type of grave marker, possibly for one of the
Knights Templar who came to the island in search of the Ark
of the Covenant. We waited as Misgana and the Aba stood
next to the cross, as we watched from a distance during their
long discussion. I'm a very anxious person, so I headed for the
temple where the sounds of the drums continued to pound out.
I pulled the shroud to the side and stared into a very large dark
room. The floor was covered in palm and banana leaves, and I
just stood there with my eyes closed listening to the sounds of
their worship. I stepped back from the door, and looked back to
see the negotiations of Misgana and the Aba were continuing.

Bob headed back over to them as they talked, and finally he returned over to us with a plain and simple "No." Bob said, "All we want to do is dig up the grave to confirm that this is who we are told it is." Misgana once again said, "No, the Aba says no." The explanation was to say that since this was considered Holy ground, we were in no way going to defile the area by digging up the remains of a body to prove a point. I walked up to Bob and said, "There's no real reason to dig, and they look at this as a holy place anyway. We probably should honor that." So, we sat the shovel along the fence, and turned to continue our trek up the cliffs.

THE DISCOVERY OF THE EVIDENCE OF THE HOLY ARK: THE FOOTHOLDS

As we turned to make our way around the temple, the tingling sensation in my body started to intensify. Maybe the drums slowly beating inside the building, the chanting of prayers, and the sun were starting to get to me. Or, at least, that's what I thought. On up the cliff, another fifty yards, where the rocks started to become very narrow, only 15 feet or so, before dropping off forty feet below into the Lake Tana waters, the feeling, just like in Axum had taken me to my limit. I dropped down to my knees on the rocks, and hit quite hard. Dave moved toward me, grabbing my collar, and stood there asking, "Are you alright?" I told him that I was, and the High Priest said to Misgana, and he translated, "In front of you is where the Ark sat when it was on the island." Where I fell was a flat slab, facing north to south. The flat slab of rock he was pointing at angled east to west. It was covered with dead grasses, dirt, leaves, and small stones, but it just happened to be where I went down. After I sat there for a minute, for whatever reason, it was like a jolt to my body, I began to quickly pull the grass, and brush away the leaves, rocks, and dirt.

Jim sitting where he collapsed with the Ark of the Covenant footholds to the right.

Almost immediately I saw a small round indention in the slab measuring approximately two and a half inches in diameter. As I kept looking, I saw another about a twenty two inches across, extending from the first one, measuring the same two and a half inches. I didn't have a clue what was there, but something was, and I pointed to the indentions in the stone.

Pointing to one of the carved footholds of the Ark of the Covenant.

This was the exact spot that the Holy Ark of the Covenant was said to have rested for hundreds of years, but evidently no one had ever cleared off the grass and dirt before. It was evident that something had been sitting there as I continued to move the debris and clear the area. The High Priest dropped down to his knees and looked up to Misgana and said, "Those would be the holes to hold the feet of the Ark in place." He stood by to see what I uncovered. My thoughts were running wild. How and why did God lead me this place? I handed my camera to Steve Inman, and asked him to shoot video while I attempted to find the other two markings, or foot-holds for the Ark. As I knelt in the place of the Ark, I couldn't help the tears that were freely flowing down my face. There was something about that spot, that place, and I wasn't sure what it was. If this was truly where the Ark rested, there had to be at least two more indentions, and their measurements would have to be close to the measurements of the Ark, depending upon their placement on the bottom. I continued to pull weeds, and throw them out to the side, and there was another mark just over three and half feet from the upper indention, and one centered between them. But, where were the others? Finally, I pulled up a thick piece of grass that was covering a portion of the stone, and there they were. About a foot and a half across was the fourth marking, and another centering between it and the first one I found, just as on the other side. There was also one in the center of the rectangular off box on the stone. I now felt the statement that I had heard just a little while earlier, as it was flashing like bright lights through my mind, "You now walk on holy ground."

During all of this, Bob continued to show the group the Holy of Holies pole hole he discovered many years earlier. There was one pole hole behind me, out to the west, and another about thirteen and a half feet from the first. These were where the poles were set for the tabernacle's Holy of Holies to cover the Ark. A small tin building sat on the cliff-side just a few feet away, and inside were two more pole settings that had broken off the cliff centuries earlier. They had located them in the waters below, cut them from the rock, and they put them in the shed, which also contained the stone bowl that the high priest would put the blood of the sacrifice in for the atonement of sin in the presence of God. The high priest, dressed in yellow, whose name was Gabriel, knelt next to me on the stone slab, and we gazed at the footholds, as I pulled out a tape measure. Dave knelt down, and we measured the markings, and without surprise, but still in amazement, they measured the dimensions of the biblical Ark of the Covenant. The Aba Gabriel stood up and demonstrated the sprinkling of the blood with his horsehair whip. He snapped first toward the top where the Ark would have rested, and then to the ground below. I asked, "Why on the ground?" Misgana replied "That is where the soles of God's feet would rest." Then I remembered the passage where God says:

> *"And he said unto me, Son of man, the place*
> *of my throne, and the place of the soles of my*
> *feet, where I will dwell in the midst of the chil-*
> *dren of Israel for ever, and my holy name,"*
> (Ezekiel 43:7)

Jim measuring the dimensions of the footholds, matching the Ark of the Covenant's biblical measurements.

He said to Misgana to tell me, "Only God could have sent you to find these, in this place. These are the holdings of the Ark of God." I felt a comfort as he put his hand on the middle of my back, as he stood watching over my shoulder at these new-found discoveries that change everything about their claims. It wasn't me, though, it was God Who lead my hands to each of these.

WHERE JESUS KNELT WITH HIS FATHER

Top: Stone bowl where the priest would dip into for the blood of sacrifice on the Ark of the Covenant's Mercy Seat.
Bottom: Pole holes for the Holy of Holies tent.

117

After inspecting closely, the sacrificial stone bowl and pole indentions, we made our way on up the cliff. I glanced down at what appeared to be another indention in the rocks on the edge of the west side of the cliff. When I went back down to my knees, I grabbed hold of the edge, where the indention was, and it broke off into my hand as I dug my fingernails into the rock with my left hand to keep from falling off. Even though there was a ledge just below, I still didn't want to run any risk of tumbling on down to the waters. If the fall didn't kill me, the inhabitants of the waters would definitely take care of me. I threw the piece of rock into my bag, which had fallen off my shoulder, and was hanging over the cliff, and pulled myself up with a clump of grass. After I lifted myself back to my feet, I decided to move onward to a pair of large boulders on the left side of the pathway. Between the boulders, smaller watermelon-sized rocks were stacked high. One of the monks said that is where the Levite priest who brought the Ark to Tana Kirkos was buried, and his remains lay under those rocks still today. Think of it, the body of the actual Levite priests who came from Aswan, in Egypt, with the Ark of the Covenant, lay in a very humble grave just inches in front of me. After the others in the team passed by, I climbed up the backside of one of the boulders and looked down inside the tomb. Although I couldn't see anything inside, I'll trust their claim that this was also a very holy site in the trail of the Ark. I then went up another thirty feet and the monk once again said that this was the ledge where the Ark was lifted from the water, some sixty or more feet below, to this cliff where it rested in hiding.

I stepped back for a second to take in all that was around me: Holy ground, the Ark's resting place covered by a tabernacle, the high priests of the Levites buried between two boulders, and the lifting site where the Ark was hoisted for safety on this incredible remote island. It was almost overwhelming to take it all in, but even more incredible was to realize the tremendous divine history with the shroud of mystery that surrounded this particular land I stood upon, and the presence of God in this spot. But for some reason, the Ark and the thought that we were passing upon holy ground just would not leave my consciousness. I didn't know what was going on inside my head. It just seemed like there was more. There had to be more. There was something that I was still missing. There had to be something that I had missed, or just had not found in my search as of yet.

I made my way down the cliff again to the site where I had found the footholds hidden away in the grass and debris. I knelt down again and just couldn't believe that these had been hidden here, and no-one had cleaned the area until now to prove the claim of the island's high priest. While I knelt there, I once again measured the markings, and there was no doubt that they were the same size of the Ark. Seven carvings into the stone, six in a somewhat perfect rectangle, and one in the center.

The 7 footholds of the Ark of the Covenant with lines added to help give proportions to the box.

As I sat there, Aba Gabriel knelt down again next to me as I asked him a question about why there were seven instead of just four. He said to Misgana to translate, "The Ark was made of wood with heavy gold around it. It was filled with the stone law of God, and a very heavy gold top, the chair of God, made of gold. The center of the Ark would have broken, that's why the two holes on the center sides and then one in the middle." He said that he had always heard this, but never had seen them to prove that before now. It was just more of a confirmation that these were truly the placements of the Throne of God! Aba said something to Misgana, and he turned to me and said, "Tell him that where you are kneeling is where Jesus knelt." I turned around my head, with my knees still planted firmly on the rock and said, "What did you say?" The Aba said, "That when Jesus was a boy He knelt where you are with His Father at the Ark." He motioned for us to come with him.

Tears began to roll down my face while still being in a bit of a shock. Dave walked up and wanted to know if I knew what the Aba was talking about, so, I went over it with him while I sat there still in a state of amazement. Confusion rattled inside my head as I sat there for a moment on the exact spot where God Himself rested His feet, and now something to do with Jesus actually coming to this place to pray on this slab of rock as well. If what I heard was truth, the place where I am resting on my knees would actually be the only place on earth that both God the Father and God the Son would have ever met. And since Jesus had not yet been to the cross, the power that was within the Ark was that of the Holy Spirit. So, in reality, this would have been the place of all three at that one time.

Think about it, a remote island, guarded from the world, and inhabited by only monks who are chosen for their purity, and glaring with their dedication to faith. Could this possibly be the most Holy spot on earth, or at least a rival to the top spot? I collected my thoughts, and made some notes and drawings in my journal about the resting place of the Ark. Then Dave grabbed my hand and pulled me up as we followed the Aba back down the cliff, past the temple, and through the rock archway to meet up with those who had already ventured back and missed the shocking announcement. God was in the midst of opening up a revelation, and I prayed that I was prepared to take it all in, without losing any of it.

Ancient treasury building on Tana Kirkos Island. Note the large python skin above the doorway.

After clearing the archway and leaving the place considered to be "Holy ground," I put my shoes back on and we followed the Aba to the small stone treasury building nestled between the archway, the cliffs, and the jungle. As Aba went to collect the sets of keys to unlock a very heavy wooden door with three large extremely old locks keeping the contents concealed from the world, the thought of Jesus kneeling here may be the big missing piece of the puzzle. While the Aba was gone, Misgana said to follow him up the higher cliffs to see the incredible view. As the temperatures were rising, and the sun was at its peak in the sky barreling down on us, Misgana led me up the cliff to the highest point, to the top of the rock. He pointed down below where the old stone treasury was located, and told me that this is where Jesus would play and they would eat. I put my head down to regain my composure, and then looked back up to Misgana and asked, "So, what you're telling me is that Jesus Christ was actually on this island when he was a boy. He was really here?" "Yes," he said. "The Aba will show you down there."

Could this actually be the place where some two thousand years ago, that Jesus came to meet with His Father, upon the Ark, or the throne? If this is the place, it appears to be the perfect setting for such a truth. From this point, I could see everything: an undefiled piece of rock and earth that was created by God to be the site from the beginning of time to host a heavenly conference. I can see the other side of the island where the women had to stay back. I can see for miles over the lake to the non-inhabited shoreline of the mainland. Islands in all directions could be seen in a variety of shapes and sizes. But the most important sites in the vision from this high rock cliff is the place where all three of the Godly Trinity met here on earth. Never before has there ever been such a place below heaven that all three met, other than the Garden of Eden, in the midst where God walked with Adam.

Then it clicked, I felt like I was beginning to get the purpose behind this power summit. But realizing that more needed to be researched; I grabbed my Bible from my backpack and quickly opened up to Luke chapter two. I remember from reading this chapter many times over the years, two verses of Scriptures that, for some reason, just resurfaced to my brain. I have read this before but it never materialized into anything I felt I needed to adhere to because of the main stories that bookend this line. Of course, preceding this single line is the Christmas story and then it is followed by Jesus' disappearance with Mary and Joseph going back to find Him in Jerusalem teaching in the temple at the age of twelve. But then, you always hear about testimony of people saying they have read Scripture over and over again, but not understanding it or not paying attention to it until God needs you to. I think that is what may have happened here. I have read and passed it by many times before. Luke says in his gospel:

> *"And when they had performed all things according to the law of the Lord... And the child grew, and waxed strong in spirit, filled with wisdom: and the grace of God was upon him."*
> (Luke 2:39-40)

This was after the holy family had returned from Egypt and all of the customary rituals had been completed. Could this be the clue that led us to this remote island in Ethiopia in the middle of Lake Tana? We may be resting in the very spot where Jesus and God the Father met in order to fulfill this Scripture. This Scripture reveals to us that Jesus, God in the flesh, was brought to be strong in His Spirit, and filled with the wisdom and knowledge to prepare Him for what was to come with God's grace upon Him. It started to sink into my simple

124

mind that God might be clearing a path, and slowly opening me up to a revelation about Luke 2:40, and offering the "when" that Jesus received His wisdom from God, and "where" that this grace was placed upon Him. It also fulfills the Scripture of the Prophet Isaiah in chapter seven, where it tells us that the coming Messiah will be somewhat, weaned into knowing what He would have to do to accomplish His purpose upon this Earth:

> *"Therefore the Lord himself shall give you a sign;*
> *Behold, a virgin shall conceive, and bear a son,*
> *and shall call his name Immanuel. Butter and*
> *honey shall he eat, that he may know to refuse*
> *the evil, and choose the good. For before the*
> *child shall know to refuse the evil, and choose*
> *the good, the land that thou abhorrest shall be*
> *forsaken of both her kings."* (Isaiah 7:14-16)

Tana Kirkos Island was possibly the place of a great meeting. This could very well be the place where The Son was filled with all that was needed for what was to come.

As I stood there with watery eyes, a spiritual feeling washing over me, I turned around to look at the awe-inspiring view over Lake Tana, and started thinking to myself, "Could this possibly be the ending stop for Jesus to meet with His Father in privacy to receive instruction for an entire lifetime of direction, and all knowledge, and strength to face the many events to come in His life?" I stared out over the lake, off in the distance, was a very deserted but lush green coast line of Lake Tana. Misgana, who had wandered farther on the cliff, returned to me and said, pointing to the mainland, that is where Joseph (Jesus' earthly father) stayed and farmed the ground for food and money. I asked, "How can this be? The Bible says nothing of Jesus coming here." He replied, "There's much the Bible doesn't tell you. But, you will see (pointing back down to the building) that it is true, Jesus was here. Jesus was here as a boy with His Father."

THE ISLAND TREASURY

I made my way down the cliff, climbing over drying coffee beans, and went straight to treasury door. Aba Gabriel was opening the door, as I followed him and Bob inside. Bob said, "I told him that you are a holy man from America." At that time, I was a pastor in a church, but I believe I had already begun to win the trust of Aba Gabriel. I watched as Aba braced the door so we could see inside from the bright sun outside. Thrill, adventure, anticipation and confusion were all encompassing me at that very moment, unsure of whether to cry, argue, or fall on my face in prayer. I just stood there with an overwhelming Spirit over me as I felt like something was beginning to change in my life.

This treasury was just one room, but many of us packed in while the others stood in the doorway. There was a musty smell to the inside, but there was some dust and a dirt floor with a carpet thrown over it. To the right and in front was shelf after shelf of ancient scrolls, books, and parchments. To the left, upon makeshift wood and bamboo shelves, were what appeared to be a treasure trove of dusty artifacts that only the Aba knew for sure what they were. The Aba handed Bob a cage-looking piece of pounded metal. He handed it to me and said it was the remains of the breastplate harness of the high priest for the tabernacle atonement ceremony. The Aba pointed and mumbled some words as in reference to the piece. He went on to explain that the Ephod of the high priest that contained the twelve stones of the twelve tribes of Israel would have be laid over and attached to this harness.

Then the Aba showed us a large aged metal bowl.

This was the bowl where the priest would have cleansed himself before entering the presence of God in the Holy of Holies. A crumbling metal stand, next to us and resting on the ground, was the piece that the bowl sat upon. Due to the age and weight of the bowl, the stand had nearly collapsed. Then

Aba Gabriel holds the ancient bowl for cleansing for the Ark ceremony.

the items just kept coming, one after another. Next were meat forks with almond bud designs on the top. These were the forks that held the sacrificial meat for the burnt offerings, and the almond was the sign from Aaron, Moses' brother, serving as the high priest. It was Aaron's almond staff that God made to bud and flower that was included inside the Ark of the Covenant. This, again, was a sign of these items truly coming from the time of Moses, continuing on to Solomon's temple, and then to Tana Kirkos. Aaron's symbol of the almond was just another piece of the puzzle that didn't have to be shown, but was confirmation

Ancient meat fork used to hold meat over the fire for the burnt offering of the sacrifice. Note Aaron's almond bud symbol at the top.

of what we were seeing as truth to the claims of the monks.

There were ancient shofar horns, incense burners, additional meat hooks for hanging the meat in order to collect the blood for sacrifice, and a variety of other items. I've read accounts of the Egyptians opening up crypts and finding a slew of ancient and historical artifacts. This was much the same, but we didn't have to become tomb raiders to find these artifacts. It was like a biblical museum in a hut made of rock and mud, covered with a tin and thatched roof.

There had to be some merit to all this. There was little to no metal at all on this island. Everything for the most part is made of wood, reed, or rock. Where did they get these things? Are they truly from Solomon's temple? Misgana, translating for the Aba, said, "These are all from Solomon's Temple and came to the island with the high priest who brought the Ark here." This, of course, is the same high priest whose body lies under the rocks farther up the cliff-side. I had to ask, "Then why are they still here? The Ark and the trumpets of silver are in Axum, so why are these pieces still here?" The Aba, through Misgana, explained, "King Ezanus came here with his army and said that the Ark belonged in his kingdom in Axum. They were now Christians and believed in Jesus, so they did not take anything for the sacrifice because they did not need it there." I questioned, "So, all the blood sacrificial items like the breastplate, meat forks and gomer were left here?" He said, "Yes. They did not need them anymore because they were Christian and Jesus had come, so no sacrifice was needed anymore."

It all started to make sense now. The Ethiopian King only took with him the needed pieces of the treasury. The trumpets of Moses traveled with the Ark everywhere it went to announce its arrival. Then, of course, the Ark itself went to Axum, and they claim it continues to rest there today in the St. Mary of Zion church. Our team appeared to be like detectives looking and investigating everything. A couple of times someone would reach for something and the Aba would raise his hand and shake his head no. In other words, "Don't touch!" Recently, the metal objects in this treasury were tested for their age, and to no surprise, they all dated to the time of the Ark's resting on this island and well beyond.

THE BOOK AND THE REVELATION

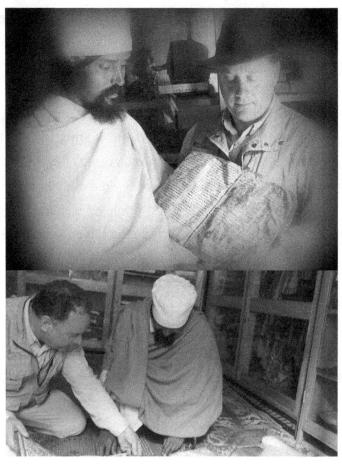

Jim and Aba Gabriel holding and studying the ancient manuscript of the early trek of Jesus and his family.

While all this was going on, I couldn't help but think about this claim of Jesus coming here as a boy. Aba Gabriel turned to Misgana and said something, and then he motioned for the men to leave the building as the Aba turned to rustle through the stacks of scrolls and animal hide books. Bob, Misgana and I stood by as the Aba seemed to have found what he was looking for. He turned toward us, and I took a deep breath and a big gulp, as Dave stepped back in. The pages of this parchment book were stiff, as it was written in some type of ink nearly 2000 years ago. I wasn't sure whether it was berry juice, or some other ink-like liquid on a thick animal hide. Pieces were literally breaking off the book and falling to the floor. Then he stopped on a page near the end of the book. The Aba pointed to the writings on the left side of the book and said, through Misgana's translation, "This book tells us that Jesus traveled here from Egypt when He was a boy to be alone with His Father." I said quickly, "Jesus came to this island?" The reply was, "Yes." I turned to Bob and asked, "How can this be? There are no writings of this at all." Bob replied, "It appears as though there are now." This sent shock waves down my spine, and I trembled. My face was flush, and I instantly felt both drained and exhilarated. I turned back and belted out, as if to quiz the priest, "How long was he here?" He went on to tell us that Jesus was here three months and ten days, and He prayed by the Ark sometimes night and day. Then his hand slid over to the right-side page that contained a beautifully drawn picture in blue, red and black ink made from berry juices and charcoal. It was a picture of a small boy, "Jesus," the Aba claimed, "His mother and two others on a small papyrus reed boat rowed out to the island." Then the following pages were opened to other incredible writings.

I asked if we could take the book outside so we could get a clearer photo of the book and its writings. The Aba agreed to take it near the door, and we moved to the outside of the building and under the bamboo and thatch covering as the sunlight exposed the beige-like pages of this book. We could see it much clearer now. The others on the team appeared just as thrilled as I was. How could we not be? Aba felt that I needed to see this because of the findings on the stone slab of the footholds of the Ark. He said, "You have been chosen as the one to see this." This has been guarded here for 1900 years and only seen, up until this point, by the monks and priests who were given privilege to see it. Aba Gabriel allowed me to take very clear photos of the book from many angles before he turned and walked inside, and placed it back inside the shelf with many other books. Little did I know, the path to completely reveal what was written in this book was being cleared. Quickly, I was going to be presented with the clear vision that this was one of those mysteries that God was opening up for the world to know.

Chapter 7:

ALONG THE PATH TO TANA KIRKOS

After studying the book, the writings inside, and the trail of the holy family, it appears as though the journey into Egypt was only the start to a much bigger adventure for Jesus. As we follow Him through Egypt, all of the Egyptian writings have Him stopping in the town of Al-Muharraq. To me, that never made sense. Why would they retreat into the southern regions of Egypt when Herod's army didn't even know who they were looking for? Why would they travel so far to the south when Herod's soldiers wouldn't have dared to travel into the Egyptian desert? The Scripture tells us that;

> *"Herod, when he saw that he was mocked of the*
> *wise men, was exceeding wroth, and sent forth,*
> *and slew all the children that were in Bethlehem,*
> *and in all the coasts thereof, from two years old*
> *and under,"* (Matthew 2:16)

When Joseph packed up the family and headed for Egypt, it was an escape from Herod's wrath in Israel, not in Egypt. It is also very possible that John the Baptist (as a child) may have also been a target since his father (Zacharias) was known in the temple. There are writings of Elisabeth retreating in the deserts with John, and Zacharias being killed in the temple. With that said, it was obvious that Herod had no idea who Jesus was. So, to compromise for his lack of information from the wise men, he ordered the slaughter of hundreds, if not thousands, of innocent young children, and dumped the bodies in what is today known as Herod's Catacombs. Besides, his men would not be a welcomed group in this African land. If they would have attempted to follow the holy family into Egypt, they wouldn't have followed very long into this blisteringly hot desert region.

As we saw before, Jesus, along with Mary and Joseph, traveled almost in a looping pattern in the northern regions of Egypt before connecting on the Nile River and heading due south. My investigative nature kicked in as I stood there on a remote island, guarded by monks, and accentuated by a clear biblical spiritual feeling surrounding it. I immediately went over and sat down on a rock under the reed boat resting on the cliff, swung my back-pack from my shoulder to the ground, and unzipped the large compartment in the front. Once again, I grabbed my Bible and looked up Matthew chapter two, and then a couple of other Scriptures telling of the Messiah in Egypt. I checked out the reference to Isaiah 19:1 as the idols fell upon the presence of the coming Messiah through Egypt:

"Behold, the LORD rideth upon a swift cloud,
and shall come into Egypt: and the idols of
Egypt shall be moved at his presence"

This tells us that when the Lord moves through, like a swift cloud through Egypt, that the idols of that nation shall be moved or fall in His presence. When Jesus moved through Egypt, all along the path, the idols and temples of pagan gods fell to the ground. Every location that describes the trail of the holy family includes these facts today in these locations. This all referred me back to Isaiah again:

"Woe to the land shadowing with wings, which
is beyond the rivers of Ethiopia: That sendeth
ambassadors by the sea, even in vessels of bul-
rushes upon the waters, saying, Go, ye swift
messengers, to a nation scattered and peeled, to
a people terrible from their beginning hitherto;
a nation meted out and trodden down, whose
land the rivers have spoiled! All ye inhabitants
of the world, and dwellers on the earth, see ye,
when he lifteth up an ensign on the mountains;
and when he bloweth a trumpet, hear ye. For so
the LORD said unto me, I will take my rest, and
I will consider in my dwelling place like a clear
heat upon herbs, and like a cloud of dew in the
heat of harvest. For afore the harvest, when the
bud is perfect, and the sour grape is ripening in

*the flower, he shall both cut off the sprigs with
pruning hooks, and take away and cut down the
branches. They shall be left together unto the
fowls of the mountains, and to the beasts of the
earth: and the fowls shall summer upon them,
and all the beasts of the earth shall winter upon
them. In that time shall the present be brought
unto the LORD of hosts of a people scattered
and peeled, and from a people terrible from
their beginning hitherto; a nation meted out and
trodden under foot, whose land the rivers have
spoiled, to the place of the name of the LORD
of hosts, the mount Zion."* (Isaiah 18:1-7)

This Scripture describes Ethiopia perfectly. Remember,
at the time of Isaiah, Ethiopia was a building empire. The
Scripture clearly points to an Ethiopia that has suffered and
has changed little over time. Both the lands and people are suffering. It talks about the mountains and how a sign will be seen
coming from them. In Ethiopia, these northern regions are the
mountainous regions of the country: Axum, Gondar, Lalibela,
Barhir Dar and yes, the island of Tana Kirkos. It describes them
traveling in bulrush or reed boats, and how one day a very
special "present" will be brought from Ethiopia to the Lord of
hosts, Jesus, when He takes up His new kingdom on the throne
in Jerusalem in the Holy of Holies in the temple. We know that
gift as His throne, the Mercy Seat, which the priests in Axum
claim they have, and the entire country believes it as well.

I then glanced back at Luke 2:40 one more time, just to make sure that there was an event that took place where Jesus was fulfilled with all that He was about to do. I walked back over to the treasury and looked in where Gabriel had put the book in with other historical writings, but it had seemed to have disappeared into the shelf. I yearned to spend the day just holding and meditating about this book. Is it possible that this is untold history? Possibly another secret hidden away in Ethiopia for centuries until it was time to be brought forth? Could it be a historical account of Jesus in a preset meeting with His Father to prepare Him for His ministry upon this Earth? If discernment can be trusted, this was exactly the feeling I was getting. There was a supernatural sense about this place. It was a feeling that I had never experienced before, and it felt as though my thoughts were not coming from me, but rather given to me to document and prepare for the world to receive.

TIME TO LEAVE THE ISLAND

Even though I felt I could have stayed there for days on end, we made our way back through the jungle to the cliff opening where the ladies were anxiously waiting for our return. Before we left the island, there was still much to do for the monks who had assembled to join us. Many of these men were very old with many ailments due to lack of medical attention. Since they don't leave the island, they don't get the proper care they need when illness or pains arise. After giving them ointments and pain medications, Kathryn and Dr. Sue took cheek swabs of the two older monks. These men claim to be from the Levite sect, and we wanted to get some of their DNA in order to try to squelch any doubt that we or anyone else may have.

We also spent some time mingling with the monks, exchanging gifts, and taking part in the custom of drinking coffee. I have to admit that I am not a coffee drinker and this concoction confirmed the reason why. It was simply awful, but who am I to judge! Sherri took off her bracelet that I had given her for Christmas that shares the plan of salvation through Christ and gave it to one of the women on the island. These women come over from the mainland to the top of the cliff to cook for these monks next to a mud and thatch building. Sherri tried to explain to them that it was a bracelet telling the life of Jesus Christ, and that He died for our sins. They shook their heads as if they understood as many can understand English but can't speak it.

Some of the medical supplies we carried with us were used on some of the monk's eyes, as well as a variety of skin irritations that they had. We gave horsehair fly swatters to a couple of the men, too. After some final traditional Ethiopian handshakes and goodbyes, we began to make our way down the slippery cliff side once more. Before Sherri and I made our way down, we walked to the opposite edge of the cliff. It was a fifty foot drop straight down, and we could see birds nesting in their little mud homes, and the waters of Lake Tana splashing up against the rock walls. I glanced around the island one more time, and stared out over the lake from that side. I said to her, "Can you imagine or even contemplate what took place on this island?

God came down from Heaven right here and met with His Son Jesus on this place." She looked at me puzzled, and I told her that I would share the whole story with her on the boat.

As we gazed out over the lake, tears welled up as I was praying to myself for God to show me something to confirm that what I had seen here was the truth, and what I was supposed to do with this revelation. We turned and I looked down on the ground and noticed, buried in the grass, a cross made of papyrus.

This was the same type of plant used to make the boat that Jesus traveled in to this island according to the ancient book that the Aba had shown me. I reached down, picked it up, and slipped it into my Bible secured in my backpack. Later I would find that the place where I had quickly inserted the cross was Isaiah 18.

To me, it was a final confirmation that I had

The papyrus cross Jim found in the dirt on Tana Kirkos Island.

come to search for the Ark of the Covenant, but somehow had ended up in the middle of the beginning of the road to the Cross for Jesus. The knowledge of His mission may have started right here on this island. This small cross made of bulrush may be God's way of saying that, "I sent you here to reveal another story to the world that it was time for them to know." A peace came over me as I put my arm around my wife with tears in my eyes. At this moment, I knew it was time for me to go, while also realizing that this wasn't the last time I would set foot on this island. I would be back here someday, because I felt that God had more to show me when I returned.

We made our way to the cliff side with the rest of our team and headed back down to the water. I turned and shook the hand of the Aba, once more. After we boarded the boat and shoved off, I took one last glance at the island with the two-large white and black eagles standing guard, and perched in the tree above the cliff where Mary rested and prayed. We waved to the monks on the rocks who made their way down the cliff to send us off as the boat's captain made a swift left turn, and we were on our way back. As I looked back, Aba Gabriel stood and nodded to me on the cliff-side, as I nodded in return and gave a slight wave to him. I was like a frazzled little kid as I attempted to tell Sherri about what we had just seen and heard "on the Holy ground." She was in awe, as were a couple of the other women, as I went through what we just had witnessed on this island piece by piece.

The ancient manuscript revealing much of the missing years of Jesus' early life and His meeting with His Father before the Throne.

I pointed up to the eagles and said, "That's the spot where Mary prayed and watched over Jesus. Right over there is where Jesus knelt in prayer with His Father at the Ark of the Covenant, where the tabernacle stood. The high priest that brought the Ark to the island is buried between those two rocks, and that cliff is where the Ark was pulled up from these waters." Sherri responded, as did Bev and Kathryn, "Jesus was here?" I said to them, "Yes, Jesus came here to be alone with His Father." We can only imagine what that period must have been like, what must have been talked about, and what came from this meeting. I believe these revelations are perfectly aligned with Scripture and fulfill many prophetic declarations, but I knew we had to have more to confirm all of this. To think, it all started right here, and the world has been hidden from knowing it for some two thousand years.

I jumped off the bow onto the walkway along the side cabin and headed to the covered awning over the back of the boat and began to research. As the motor pushed us farther across the lake, I couldn't help but think about the path that Jesus took to get onto this island. I wondered how long it took them to get there. Questions upon questions were reeling through my head, and it was time to write them down and answer them. I had studied Jesus' trek into Egypt just months earlier, but now it was more than just a study, it had become a mission. It was an Indiana Jones-type adventure, a Sherlock Holmes mystery, and a James Bond thriller all wrapped up into one. This surely did become a mission. Not just any old mission, not a fiction-alized adventure, but one of revelation to the world.

THE HOLY APPOINTMENT

As I continued to look at Jesus' trip down the Nile to Al-Muharraq, I started to really understand that this was no coincidence. Herod's soldiers were not following them that far into Egypt by any stretch of the imagination. The holy family was using the Nile as a GPS to follow the mission that God was sending them on. They were on a journey to a holy appointment between Jesus and His Father. What was the young Messiah doing on a remote island in the middle of a giant lake in the northern highlands of Ethiopia? Why was He alone, except for His mother, on top of the rocky cliffs, and the monks that guarded this island somewhere off in the distance? Could this be a coincidence that the Ark of the Covenant was resting here at the same time? Questions were streaming through my head faster than answers were coming. Then, it all started to come together and make sense, like a Rubik's Cube when the little squares start to match-up.

Best-selling author, Paul Perry, had done a tremendous amount of research, writing the book *Jesus in Egypt*, and hosted the documentary *Jesus: The Lost Years,* about the holy family's trek into Egypt *(ref. 8)*. After an interview with Paul for our *Adventures in Truth* article in a faith based magazine, I shut off the recording devices and asked him, "Why do you think Jesus and his family traveled all the way down to Deir al-Muharraq before getting the instruction to turn around and head back home?" He had no explanation or theory on that question. You see, Paul's extensive study was only on the topic of Jesus in Egypt, and he is one of the best on this subject as he traveled the entire trail of the holy family for his research. During Paul's time with the monks and priests in Deir al-Murharraq, he was told that after touching the rock that Jesus slept on, he was supposed to pray for something that he really wanted. Paul simply prayed for some confirmation that this trail of the holy family was true. He received that confirmation through a flash of light over the temple during a photo opportunity that he took later that night *(ref. 8)*. Knowing that I could trust Paul on his answer, I continued, "How do you know this was the last place they traveled to? Even though Joseph was told to come home from here, how do we know this was the last place?" Paul replied, "It appeared the trail ended here." That was the point that turned my investigation into high gear. For Paul, his mission was complete because his study was centered on Jesus during His spectacular time in Egypt. We were taking this one step further, because our adventure was turning to Jesus in Ethiopia, which until now, had not been revealed to the outside world. Was it a step of faith? Absolutely! But it was a step where every possible rock and road was placed on the path for us to follow.

This was more than just a vacation for the holy family; it was a hard, merciless trip down the crocodile-and hippo-infested Nile River through Egypt. The Nile continues south out of Egypt into Sudan, which all the territory south of Egypt in the ancient times was Ethiopia. During my study, I realized that the Nile River even went a little farther than I had first thought. I found that Lake Tana (Ethiopia), through the Blue Nile Falls, dumps right into the Blue Nile River, traveling south, swinging to the west, and then north where it meets up with the White Nile River to form the Nile River. Lake Tana is the main source to the Nile, which helps to explain the route for the holy family. They traveled to Deir al-Muharraq in Egypt, along the Nile River, straight down to the Blue Nile, and right to Lake Tana where they loaded up in a reed boat, and traveled to the island of Tana Kirkos.

There were still many questions to answer, though. I had a strong sense that most of what I was thinking would be confirmed in the pages of the ancient book that Aba Gabriel showed me on the island. If this book contained in it what I felt, then we were on the verge of a long-lost hidden secret. Not one that will change the world in Christianity, but one that will offer up a whole new look into a once thought, unrecorded time period in the life of Jesus Christ. Many questions still were unanswered, but I felt that if God's hand were in it, then He would also open up the doors and clear the paths to make the answers clearer.

Chapter 8:

LOST WRITINGS: JESUS AND THE FATHER MEET

As OUR BOAT DREW closer to the shoreline, we could see young boys pushing themselves through the water with a long wooden pole while standing upon a huge reed mat. It almost looked like a floating carpet on top of the water. Another boy passed by, without even a stitch of clothing, in a papyrus fishing boat, while another group of four men pushed their large papyrus mat along in the water with the help of a long tree branch paddle. Huge white and black cranes, along with a variety of other birds, rested in the trees, while the captain yelled out something to us in Amharic. One of his crew came running out of the cabin and pointed to two large hippos in the water. We slowed as we came closer to these two awesome giants as they watched us closely as we entered their territory. Again, hippos are very territorial, but these two didn't show much interest in us at all. I was amazed by the young boys in the boats as they passed by, since Hippos are responsible for more deaths in Africa than any crocodile. But to these boys it was like business as usual. The same held true for the hippos as they glared over at us like we were the ones on display.

We turned in closer to our dock to see dozens of citizens of Barhir Dar standing on the rocks next to the lake, washing clothes and bathing. Cormorants (a fishing bird) stood on rocks protruding from the calm waters of Lake Tana with their wings spread drying their feathers. Pelicans and a variety of other birds swooped from the sky to take in some afternoon fishing as the sun pelted down on the waters of the mighty lake. Men were waiting for us at the dock as the captain moved our boat into position to throw the ropes in for tying. We again jumped from the boat onto the dock and made our way back to our rooms. The information we had just gathered was still reeling in my head. We went back to our room, and I sat down on our bed and tried to go over everything again with Sherri. She couldn't believe what she was hearing, nor could I. This was the only evidence that the Ark had ever existed, other than what we read about in the Bible. This is just a piece of what God has revealed or will still open up in the future. The revelation to her was as powerful as the impact on me. It was information overload, and I needed to take a break from the thought for a while.

We decided to go out and walk around the town square of Barhir Dar and take in some of the sights. We came upon a small group of merchants with their wares on blankets off in the grass, just off the roadside, and we started to realize we were being pushed by a quickly building crowd. Little did we know we ended up walking right into the middle of a Muslim gathering near a mosque. Within seconds it seemed as though we had been filed in, and then pushed toward the mosque by thousands of Muslim followers. As we attempted to break away from the crowd, the trend to swallow us into the mob became somewhat overwhelming. I grabbed Sherri's collar and pushed her forcefully toward the busy roadway. I told her to not stop for the traffic, we needed to get into the road to get away from the push of the crowd. Suddenly we were in the road with the small taxis buzzing and beeping by. We jumped to the square in the middle of the circle and caught our breath. With some fear of being recognized as an obvious Christian in the mob, and being in the wrong place at wrong time, we crossed to the far side of the street and picked up a few last trinkets. This commotion was too much after our experiences earlier in the day, so we decided it was time to head back and wash up for our final dinner together as an exploration team.

The mood was festive, but the talk at the tables centered on what happened earlier in the day. After dinner, everyone wandered and relaxed around the property. Some pulled up a chair and sat in the moonlight gazing out over the calm waters of the lake for one last glance at this incredible place. Others went to their rooms to prepare for the journey the next day and to get a good night's sleep, while Sherri and I walked around the facility. Standing on the shore staring out and thinking what it must have been like when Jesus arrived here, we couldn't help but try to visualize a papyrus boat being led out across this huge expanse of water to take a young boy and His mother to a lost island. It was an island that was pure in its beginnings, and remained that way to ensure the opportunity for the holy summit between God and His Son.

Many people believe that this portion of Ethiopia was actually the site of the Garden of Eden. It would honestly make sense that God would bring His Son to the place where He created mankind in order to share with Him the purpose of His salvation for mankind from their sin. Think about it. The Garden of Eden was the place where God came down to walk with Adam. It was the place where the first sin was committed, and the place where God would share the ministry of how His Son would wash away the sin that started there. There was so much to ponder. After meeting with some of the team one last time, we made our way back to the room, packed our bags, and prepared for an early morning departure. For me, it was an open door, because God wanted reveal an important mystery, and it would also be something that God would lay the foundation for us to walk upon.

Morning arrived and we hurriedly threw our bags on top of the vans and made our way to the airport. Even the small Ethiopian airports house people trying to sell their handmade souvenirs and offer the phrase that made me laugh, "Look for free, mister." Then there are others who have hidden away older and sometimes ancient artifacts. You don't question where they came from, if it is of interest to you, just negotiate, put it in your bag, and walk away. After waiting an hour, our plane arrived to take us back to Addis Ababa. We walked out on the tarmac and boarded the turbo prop plane for the last time on this journey. As the plane barreled down the runway and with a quick pull back on the throttle, the captain lifted us up into the sky, I looked down on Lake Tana as we passed by its shores. My thought was simply, "Wow!" A place of history that has been hidden from the world for two thousand years had just revealed itself to me. Sherri could see the joy on my face, and in some way, I think it made her proud to know that we were entrusted to share this revelation with the world.

Once we landed in the capital city, it would be nearly 40 more hours before Sherri and I would finally lay our heads on our own pillows in Ohio. I didn't want to leave Ethiopia, but realized I had much more excitement to come. It was an evening flight out of Addis Ababa and a couple of our team members were detained when they attempted to get their video equipment through the government check point. They didn't get to leave with our group, but through prayer, they ended up on the next flight out. We departed and headed to Rome for a short lay-over, and then on to the fifteen-hour flight to Washington D.C., and then another eight hours driving back to Ohio. When we arrived at Dulles Airport in Washington D.C., it was somewhat congested, and we really didn't get a chance to say proper goodbyes to many of our newly found friends. But through the use of email and cell phones, we would eventually make contact with many of them again. Our team included people from Georgia, Kansas, Illinois, Iowa, California, Colorado, and Peru. Many of them continue to work with our team today, and truly have been a blessing to share this experience with. It was a great journey for all, and I pray for them often to "Arise and go" with what God shared with them on their journey.

Within a few days after returning home, I had recovered from the jet lag and begun further research, starting in Ethiopia, and then from the findings of a short list of others. I buried my head in manuscripts, church historical documents, and historical writings of Jesus' trek into Egypt. Shortly after our return, phone calls started to come in from organizations and churches that wanted to know about the journey. As a result of this interest, I hit the circuit sharing what God had led me to discover about the Ark and our newly found passion for these people of Ethiopia, while keeping the knowledge of Christ's appearance on this journey to a minimum, while continuing my research. My wife was hired by a home improvement store which was a tremendous blessing to help offset travel and living expenses, while I continued the operation of our faith-based magazine company.

TRANSLATING THE BOOK

It was a Wednesday afternoon in May 2011, Dave Kochis called me from San Francisco to discuss our plans for the return trip to Ethiopia. We strongly agreed we needed to have Bibles printed in the Amharic language to take back to the people of Ethiopia, and he wanted to know if we had any success in that translation yet. I shared what had just happened earlier in the week while attending to a funeral of a family who had lost a young child. Across the parking lot from the church was a Bible publishing company that serves numerous missionaries, so I checked with them before the services to see if they happened to have the Amharic translation of Scripture. Before going to the print shop offices, I knew that the chances were very slim that they would have this particular language because of its secluded use in Eastern Africa. This particular publishing company serves missionaries with Scripture all around the world; I knew there were none in the Amharic Ethiopian region, but I thought it would be worth the try anyway.

I stopped in and caught the director of the publishing house getting ready to leave for lunch. He was kind enough to take the time to answer a few questions and to discuss the language. He pulled out a book and flipped through it, and then turned around to his computer and said, "Let me look at another place on here." My anticipation rose as he tried to locate the language in question. Seconds seemed like minutes while his fingers continued to scroll down the pages. Finally, he turned and said, "I really don't think we've done anything like this before. I wish I could help, but I'm afraid that we don't have this translation." I was deflated. It was a flicker of light, and then a breeze blew it all out. I thanked him for his time and told him I had to go to a funeral at the church. Somewhat disheartened, I hopped into my car, drove to the church, and went into the service, realizing I needed to perk up to support the family. I was sitting in the back of the church during the service when a man tapped my shoulder, startling me from my thoughts. He leaned over and handed me a note. It read, "Al needs to see you over at the print shop." I looked at him and nodded blankly.

As the service wrapped up, I paid my respects to the family and headed out the front door. I felt like a race-car driver as I spun-out trying to return to the print shop quickly. I pulled in by their entryway, literally creating my own parking space, and headed back into the publishing company. The director was waiting for me and waved me down the hallway to his office. I walked in; he stood holding a small, green, paper covered Scripture and a floppy disk. Yes, an old floppy disk! He said, "I don't know when we would have even done this because we don't have missionaries needing this translation, but I found it." I said, "You found what?" He replied and stuttered along, "It's the Am, Amhara, no, Amharic language. We have it. I don't ever remember having this translation, but this is it on this old floppy. I found with it a translation of John and Romans as an example. I was surprised but excited to tell you. So, we can do this for you." It was like a disbelief relief. I grabbed the book from his hand and started flipping through the Scripture. Not that I could read it, but it was exciting to see. I shook his hand and said I would get a date to plan to bring a team in to print and prepare the Bibles. He agreed, we shook hands again, and I moved quickly down the hallway. It was more like a skip down the hallway, my heavy heart lightened. Finally, one phase of my search and return to this ancient land was complete!

Dave was excited that I was able to find the translation for the Bibles. He then inquired about the translation of the Bible pages from Ethiopia on Tana Kirkos Island, but I had no luck on that yet. One road after another would lead to a dead end. I just didn't want to turn the pages over to someone who had no respect for what we were trying to accomplish. These were scans of very holy documents and had been under lock and key for thousands of years. I had been entrusted with them, and I felt somewhat like a protector of the story until time to share it with the world. He then closed our conversation by saying that he was going to pray that we could find someone to translate this ancient language in its true form, and not some modern version of it. He said, "Jim, do you realize how important this information is to understanding Jesus' life as a boy and His future ministry? This has been hidden for centuries and this portion is completely unknown, if that's what it says and you can confirm it." I simply said, "I know." We ended our conversation with anxious goodbyes, knowing that it would have to be God's hand in making all of this happen.

The next day I was in Central Ohio when Sherri called me, "Jim, you have to come down here, there's a woman that started working here and she is from Addis Ababa, Ethiopia. She says she might be able to help us with the translation of the book." In disbelief, I told her I was on my way. It was about a two-hour drive to where my wife worked. I knew this could be my last shot to find someone who knew this ancient, extinct language, rather than waiting to return to Ethiopia. I waited nervously in my car until the woman, the translator, was off work. As she approached, I noticed her quickly. She had that Ethiopian smoothness to her face and a very distinctive appearance. We introduced ourselves and she said, "Let me see what you have so I can tell you what it says." I handed her the scans of the pages and she suddenly stopped. She said, "Oh...I no read this. Only an old priest can read this. No one speaks this language, and only the priests can tell you what it says." I was shaken, and it seemed my last hope for a translation had been dashed until returning to Ethiopia. Then, quite unexpectedly she added, "I think I might know someone who can read this." I said, "Who?" She quickly replied, "My priest at Ethiopian Church in Cincinnati." In shock, I stood there having no idea that an Ethiopian Church existed in Cincinnati. When she promised to ask him, I felt like hugging her but that would have been inappropriate. Instead, I grabbed her hand to shake it vigorously, and thanked her several times for taking time with me.

I called Dave in San Francisco and told him the anticipated good news, and he was elated. I belted out, "God answers our prayers when He has a mission to glorify Himself in the process, doesn't He?" Without hesitation, Dave replied, "Always. I'm so excited about this. Please keep me informed." It was about a week later when Sherri called and said she had priest's number. I called his home, but he spoke no English. A younger man picked up the phone, and although the English was much better, it was still too difficult to understand on the line. The only thing I could make out was, "We will call you." I didn't know if that was good or bad. I began to think the latter as days had gone by and I heard nothing. Then I called back and received the same answer from a woman with broken English, "We will call you" (CLICK)!

Three weeks had now passed into mid-June, and I was growing more anxious, and at the same time almost hopeless. Then, on a Wednesday morning around 8:00AM my phone rang. But when I answered no one was there. I figured if it was something important they would leave a message or call back, since I had no idea who this caller was. Thirty seconds had passed and the phone began to ring again. The man uttered in broken language, "Hello, is this Mr. Jim?" I answered expectantly as I recognized the dialect, "We will meet you today at main library, Cincinnati at 5:00PM. Bring the pages with you... goodbye." Conversation was over! I was caught in the middle of clandestine rendezvous to decipher clues about some hidden treasure. The anticipation mounted, and I called Sherri to tell her about our 5:00PM appointment.

The afternoon passed slowly by as I organized my thoughts and questions. Finally, three o'clock arrived, and we headed to Cincinnati. We first purchased a new digital voice recorder at a nearby electronics store because it was time to retire my old unreliable cassette recorder. I didn't want to risk missing a syllable during this mysterious meeting. We drove around the streets in downtown Cincinnati looking for a parking place near the library which sprawls out over two sides of the street, connected by a walkway over the busy intersection. I found an empty metered space around the corner, parked, and went in. I couldn't sit down, so we looked around and found a variety of books on Ethiopia in their wide expanse of reading. Five o'clock drew near, and I realized that sometimes these priests are uncomfortable with women present. Sherri agreed, remembering the required dawning of prayer shawls necessary while in exclusive areas of extreme holiness, and that women were not welcomed in some areas of the churches in Ethiopia. She wandered off while I stood pacing and profiling each person who entered the three entrances of the massive library. I noticed a small older man with a white beard carrying a satchel standing by the entry to the audio section, he looked Ethiopian and appeared at peace with the world, but he was alone, and the voice earlier plainly said "We will meet you." So, I knew there had to be someone else nearby if that was him, but I wasn't seeing anyone else. At that moment, my phone rang, "Mr. Jim, are you here?" came the voice both in the phone and behind me. The other much younger man with an unmistakable Ethiopian look was standing next to me. I turned in surprise and said, "It's me...I'm Jim." He then motioned to the priest, the white bearded older man to join us.

After warm handshakes and introductions, we made our way to a back-corner table to be alone. The priest took the scanned pages and began to read in a quiet voice. Yonas, the younger man, and I continued in conversation, and I expressed my thankfulness for meeting with me. He replied with the familiar simple normal Ethiopian response, "No problem." Yonas was from Addis Ababa, and the priest was from all over northern Ethiopia, but had served in Axum. Again, not surprised but another confirmation we're on the right path. Twenty minutes passed by before the older priest broke his stare from the pages, still reading under his breath. Then he turned to Yonas and spoke in the more modern Amharic. "He says, this page speaks about a meeting of like churches to settle differences and come to Egypt. God will bless them for that. This is written in a book in Alexandria library. The rest of this is not. I was momentarily disheartened as I was hoping it would contain information about Jesus in Ethiopia, when he said, "The rest of this is forever Ethiopian, like secret. No one knows the rest of this." Now they had my full attention. "Does it say anything about Jesus going to Ethiopia?" I asked. He turned to the priest and asked that question. The Aba slipped his glasses down and started to read again. It was like he wanted to make sure of what he was reading.

THE CONFIRMATION: JESUS IN ETHIOPIA

Aba Yemanebirhan looked up and spoke to Yonas, who turned to me again and said, "This writing is something no one else knows." He referred to the right side of the first page from the book, again showing nothing but the ancient hand-written language. "Aba says, this talks about Jesus, Mary, Joseph and another woman known in the Scriptures as Salome. Do you know Salome?" he asked. The Aba began to speak again as I nodded in recollection of this woman. Salome was the wife of Zebedee and the daughter of Mary's mother's sister, also named Mary, referred to in the Scriptures as "the other Mary" *(ref. 16)*. Salome is mentioned in the Bible several times including her appearance at the cross with Mary:

The ancient missing years of Jesus' early life manuscript.
Bottom: Jim with two of the translators of the ancient book of Jesus
(L to R: Dr. Rankin, Priest and translator of the book,
Unknown bishop, bystander unknown, Yonas the young man
who translated to English for the Priest.)

> *"There were also women looking on afar off:*
> *among whom was Mary Magdalene, and Mary*
> *the mother of James the less and of Joses, and*
> *Salome;"* (Mark 15:40)

And then it goes on to describe who her importance in verse 41:

> *"Who also, when he was in Galilee, followed him,*
> *and ministered unto him."* (Mark 15:41)

Then again:

> *"And when the sabbath was past, Mary Magdalene,*
> *and Mary the mother of James, and Salome, had*
> *bought sweet spices, that they might come and*
> *anoint him."* (Mark 16:1)

Salome was also John and James' mother and it was her who went to Jesus, asking for preference for her sons:

> *"Then came to him the mother of Zebedee's chil-*
> *dren with her sons, worshipping him, and desiring*
> *a certain thing of him. And he said unto her, What*
> *wilt thou? She saith unto him, Grant that these*
> *my two sons may sit, the one on thy right hand,*
> *and the other on the left, in thy kingdom. But*
> *Jesus answered and said, Ye know not what ye*
> *ask."* (Matthew 20:20a)

This clearly was Salome's request to Jesus, but it is also seen as Jesus chastises her for her asking. All-in-all, this is completely new-found information that Salome was with the holy family during this trek. This may explain her obedience to Christ throughout the Scriptures and even until His crucifixion on the cross. She was definitely a part of His life because of her relationship to Mary since He was born. This young mother asked Salome to join them on their journey to help with her Son during this strenuous trip through Egypt. I then recalled several ancient Egyptian paintings of the family's trek into this country, while they all had another woman depicted trailing behind them. Again, this is new information which plays an important role in understanding the complete historical account of this journey.

Yonas turned to me and said, "All of them traveled into Egypt after Joseph was visited by the angel, you know, that told them to leave Israel to escape Herod's killing of the children." The priest continued to speak, and Yonas continued to translate. The information was plentiful. He then said something that would really catch my attention. "This book was written by Saint John; the Apostle John was told this from Saint Mary, and his own mother who was with them, and written down by the student of Saint John. They told him about it later" he said. Excitedly I belted out, "John wrote this story from Mary and Salome's recollection?" Yonas calmly replied, "Yes, Saint John wrote this, and he tells of them going to Egypt to escape from Herod killing all the children. It says here 8,000 children, but maybe more because the page is messed up." It's amazing to think that John had a personal audience with two eyewitnesses, Mary and Salome, to most all of the life of Jesus. We know that when Jesus was on the cross He called out to John to care for His mother after He was gone. This confirms John's writings again in his gospel in verse 21:25.

Yonas continued by sharing another bit of awakening information in the book, "It says they traveled through Egypt with help of the archangel Uriel." I continued, "Is this the angel that came to Joseph to tell him to flee?" "I don't know" he said, "It doesn't tell us here." Uriel was one of the four archangels (Michael, Gabriel, Uriel and Raphael) whose name literally means the "Fire of God" or the "Light of God" *(ref.17)*. As Jesus is *"the Light,"* it makes sense that the reference to an angel guiding them with a name meaning "The Light of God" would come into play.

Yonas continued to translate from the Aba's readings, "It says here that Saint Mary and Salome told Saint John about their trip in Egypt and down to Ethiopia. This part here (pointing his finger at the etched drawing of the holy family with the angel) tells about them coming into Ethiopia; Mary, her Son Jesus, Joseph and the other lady, Salome with the angel Uriel. This says that they went together to Lake Tana in Ethiopia with the help of two men paddling on a papyrus boat, and this is the church" (pointing to a picture etched on the page of drawings). I cautiously sought confirmation, "Where is this church?" He said, "The church in Lake Tana." I shocked them with my next question, "Is this the tabernacle, or the Holy of Holies, that was on Tana Kirkos Island where the Ark of the Covenant was?" Both Yonas and the priest turned and looked at each other, and then Yonas said, "You know Tana Kirkos?" "Yes, I've been there and that's where I took these pictures of the book from." The Aba raised his head in agreement, stroked his beard, and said something to Yonas. He turned around to me and said, "Then you know that this picture is Maria, Jesus, Joseph, Salome, the angel Uriel in a boat going to Tana Kirkos to be with God?" My heart quickened as I replied, "I wasn't sure, but I was hoping that was what you were going to tell me."

Yonas continued, "This is the church (he paused and listened to the Aba for a moment), the place where Jesus would go to pray with God." I came back with the question, "Again, do you mean the tabernacle where the Ark of the Covenant was at?" Yonas nodded and then answered, "Yes, the church is like a tent or yes, the tabernacle on Tana Kirkos." The tone of the conversation began to change a little, and I wasn't sure whether it was a good or a bad change at first. But it seemed as though they began to talk with me a little more freely. Yonas stated, "This has been a secret in Ethiopia for two thousand years and few people know about this, about Jesus and Maria coming to this place." I nodded to confirm that I completely understood. It was now more evident than at any other point that God had maneuvered information into my hands for a reason. I believe that these men were sent to me to confirm that all that I had prayed about and experienced was recorded on these pages.

The priest went on, translating to Yonas, "This book was brought to Ethiopia, to Tana Kirkos by John's student, I think you say Prochorus. It is important secret of Tana Kirkos. This is the place where Jesus and Saint Mary go to be with His Father." Prochorus is noted in the Scriptures as being one of the seven deacons that were hand- picked to take care of the poor, and to continue to spread the Word of God.

> *Wherefore, brethren, look ye out among you*
> *seven men of honest report, full of the Holy*
> *Ghost and wisdom, whom we may appoint over*
> *this business. But we will give ourselves contin-*
> *ually to prayer, and to the ministry of the word.*
> *And the saying pleased the whole multitude:*
> *and they chose Stephen, a man full of faith and*
> *of the Holy Ghost, and Philip, and Prochorus,*
> *and Nicanor, and Timon, and Parmenas, and*
> *Nicolas a proselyte of Antioch: Whom they set*
> *before the apostles: and when they had prayed,*
> *they laid their hands on them.* (Acts 6:3-5)

Prochorus is said to have been the nephew of Stephen, and he traveled with the Apostle Peter during his early ministry *(ref. 18)*. Sometime later, it has been recorded that he was a student of John and became a scribe for him.

Prochorus scribing for the Apostle John.

John ordained him to become the bishop of the church in Nicomedia, and it is recorded that Prochorus was banished to Patmos with John. It is also believed that Prochorus may have been the man responsible for scribing John's vision for the Book of Revelation *(ref. 19)*. He eventually left Patmos and continued to share the gospel of Christ before suffering the death of a martyr *(ref. 20)*.

Yonas asked about the next page of the book which consisted of only eight and half lines. He asked me if this was in the beginning or end of the book, and I told him that it followed these pages. The Aba nodded his head to confirm that I was telling him the truth. This page was supposed to follow the other pages. He explained, "When Saint John wrote this down from Mary telling him about the travel here, he is telling anyone who reads this not to take out, put in, or change anything in the book because God will not be with them. He will not bless them. Their name will be removed from His book." I said, "We have this written by John in the book of Revelation." He agreed, "Yes. Yes. This says not to change the words or do anything to change what it means, just like Revelation, but this was written first before that in Revelation by John, and scribed by Prochorus."

This revealing information of who brought this information to Ethiopia fills in another piece to the puzzle, as Prochorus being the connection to the same warning from John in Revelation 22, and in the eight and a half lines in this writing:

For I testify unto every man that heareth the
words of the prophecy of this book, If any man
shall add unto these things, God shall add unto
him the plagues that are written in this book:
And if any man shall take away from the words
of the book of this prophecy, God shall take
away his part out of the book of life, and out

*of the holy city, and from the things which are
written in this book.* (Revelation 22:18-19)

After we had finished going through the text, I then went
back to the drawing of Mary, Jesus, Salome, Uriel and presumably Joseph sitting on a chair and asked what exactly they
were doing, and what this writing said. I had forgotten what
Misgana had told me on the cliff, next to the site where Mary
had watched Jesus pray at the tabernacle, that Joseph was not on
the island with them. He had told me that Joseph was working
as a farmer on the mainland to earn money for their travels.
That led to the assumption that Mary, Jesus, and Salome were
on the island, taken care of by the monks who stood guard over
the island. Yonas turned to the Aba, and they conversed for a
few minutes. Then Yonas said, "This is God holding the law
and teaching Jesus for later. He is at the church, or the tabernacle like you say, on the seat teaching Jesus all He will need."
"The seat" I asked? "Yes, the seat, (he paused to gather words)
the Ark where God would come." I was speechless. I actually
had to gather my thoughts and force myself to breathe again.
Everything was coming to light, and I really had no more questions. This was beyond everything I had hoped. Everything was
now confirmed, down to the last detail. Everything I had been
told, and everything I had experienced on the island was veri-
fied by these two incredible gentlemen.

Sitting at the table, trying to absorb this revealing information, after nearly two hours of questions, the Aba seemed to be
getting tired reading the pages. However, he told me about the

last page of the photo scan that talked about the fallen angels before Creation, and how ninety-nine angels had driven them out of Heaven. Then the Aba scooted back in his chair, as if to say, "We are done." I stood up and had to ask two more questions. First, I asked, "Do you believe that the Ark of the Covenant is in Axum?" The Aba, understanding most spoken English but unable to respond in English, nodded while Yonas answered, "Of course it is!" To question that truth suddenly seemed silly. My second question, "Do you really believe that Jesus and Mary came to Ethiopia?" Without hesitation, he answered, "There is no question they were in Ethiopia. This book tells us that He was there, and the world clouds with the tradition but is very true. Outside does not want Jesus in Ethiopia, but it is true. You see it here with your eyes." The priest talked with Yonas again, and he turned to me with even more revelation, "There were two of these books in the beginning. One was burned in the Alexandrian Library, while the other was brought to Tana Kirkos to hide away. This is the truth and it cannot be disputed." He then finished by saying, "When on Lake Tana it was very important for them. They went to Tana Kirkos to be with God."

Yonas pleasantly extended his hand to shake mine, with his other hand gripping his forearm in the traditional Ethiopian handshake. I did the same in affirmation with their custom. The same was done with the Aba, along with a slight bow to acknowledge the mutual respect we have for one another. We continued our conversation walking through the building to the front door of the library where Sherri stood waiting anxiously to hear the result of our meeting. We talked for a while as Yonas invited us to their Ethiopian church in downtown Cincinnati for an upcoming celebration a little over month away. Sherri and I both shook hands with both men and parted ways. I was truly exhausted, but thrilled with the overwhelming confirmation wrought during this secret rendezvous in the city. It was a confirmation that brought life to pages of the book with the Ark of the Covenant, God's presence, Salome, Prochorus, and the Apostle John once again as the Revelator. But most of all, we see that this small lost island was the place where Jesus and His family traveled to gain knowledge from His Father, so He could return home with God's grace, wisdom, and knowledge of His full purpose on this Earth. Again, it was after this meeting that they returned home and Jesus was astonishing the men of the church at the age of twelve. Tana Kirkos is a perfect island in many ways, and it has been kept in a purity from much of the outside world for thousands upon thousands of years.

Thinking about this even further, it truly brings to life the words written in the book of John where Jesus says that God gave Him the words to speak:

> *"For I have not spoken of myself; but the Father which sent me, he gave me a commandment, what I should say, and what I should speak."*
> (John 12:49)

This is telling us that God gave Jesus the words to say and speak, and you can't help but think this is a later confirmation of what He was taught by His Father on Tana Kirkos Island nearly two thousand years prior to us discovering this hidden truth. This was also a confirmation that God had cleared this path for me to follow, and I was not about to lay it down and let it pass by now. It confirmed for me that it was time to "Arise and go!"

Chapter 9:

CONFIRMATIONS IN STONE

AFTER MY MEETING WITH the priest and his young protégé, it was time to begin planning another return to the island. But much research had to be done in the meantime. Sherri told me that I needed to get back there, but without a group. One of our friends from the trip called me and said, "When are you going back?" We knew it had to happen, but timing and money became the issue at that time. It seemed like the funds just happened. It was like I was supposed to be on a plane to Ethiopia. I scheduled the flight and began planning our trip. I had several things I needed to explore, but the primary point was to return to Tana Kirkos and do more research. The night before I made the return to Ethiopia, Sherri and I went out to dinner with some friends before I had to leave my wife behind and begin the overnight journey to Washington D.C., arriving just in time to catch the morning flight to Ethiopia.

The flight to Africa was the normal twelve and half hours, and it went by quickly as I grabbed some sleep, and spent the rest of the time going through notes and planning the key needs to investigate while there. As the plane touched down in Addis Ababa, I grabbed my bags, and my Ethiopian friend Isaac was waiting outside in the parking lot. We stopped by Misgana's office and visited with him and his wife, before heading back to the hotel to get a good night's sleep.

Early the next morning I grabbed a quick breakfast, and Misgana was there to pick me up to catch our flight to Bahir Dar. For whatever reason, it was a tense feeling knowing that I was heading back to this island that now held a whole new meaning for me. The plane landed, and Misgana exited quickly to have our driver get the van opened up for us. We went to the motel and really just used the night to get all of our plans in order, and to enjoy a nice meal before our adventure the next day.

The eagle that guards the platform of the Ark of the Covenant and one of the Nile crocodiles you may see looming in the waters.

A TREK TO THE HOLY ISLAND

Early the next morning Misgana and I grabbed a bite to eat and made our way out to the dock to meet with Misgana on a smaller boat than in February for our journey to Tana Kirkos. There was a morning breeze and a little fog over the lake, which was fitting for the mystery of the research. The three-hour trip went by quickly as we pulled up to the island. There were a couple of the monks along the water washing their clothes, and a six-foot Nile crocodile swayed through the papyrus reeds off to the right. You could already hear the two-large white and black eagles screeching way up on the island near the area of the footholds of the Ark. We stepped from the boat onto the slick rocks, while trying to keep balance to a more, sure footing. Misgana was close behind me as we made our way, following one of the monks up the cliff side.

This time it seemed to be much different than when we had arrived here the last time. There were just a couple the monks at the top, and Aba Gabriel was not to be seen. Misgana took the lead as we made our way through the jungle arriving at the stone treasury and the rock archway, and finally, to the place of the Ark. Misgana went into a small building and asked where Gabriel was, and one of the monks pointed to the old temple. We sat on the stone step in front of the treasury building as we waited. The eagles were screeching loudly above us while you could hear other birds and sounds that you would expect in a jungle. Finally, Aba Gabriel stepped out of the temple and made his way to the treasury to greet us. He walked straight to me and embraced me rather than the traditional handshake, and did the same to his friend, Misgana.

We shared that we had gotten a translation of the book he allowed me to take the photos of, and the story was just amazing. Gabriel responded, "Mr. Jim, God sent you here, and now He will show you much more." I told him, "Thank you Aba. I really wanted to get some more photos of the book, and to study the footholds of the Ark a little closer." He replied, "Yes, we see the book first, then we go to the place of the Ark, and I have something else to show you."

He unlocked the large wooden door to the treasury, and we followed him into the dark room. Another monk opened the door wide to allow light to shine in. He went on to explain that there were many books hidden away in this place, some that aren't even in plain view, but they were here. Some were just a few decades old, and some were centuries and centuries old. He showed us closer looks at the crowns of kings, and priest's robes inside one of the cases, and then he pulled out a couple of ancient Hebrew gowns that were left here nearly a thousand years earlier. When he touched them, they simply began to fall apart.

THE CROSS OF YARED

The Aba then turned to the case next to where the book we were seeking was housed. He pulled from a shelf a folded case. As he opened it, my eyes grew wide to see a beautiful large cross perfectly fitted inside the indention inside. It was made of bronze and was very ornate and awe-inspiring. He handed it to me to hold as I asked, "What is it?" He sat the case on the shelf and said, "This is the cross of St. Yared of Ethiopia. He was born in Axum and was the priest who wrote the Ethiopian music in the church here today." I simply looked at him and said, "Wow, this is a piece of history."

Yared was, like the Aba said, born in Axum, and was sent to be raised by his uncle, Gidewon, after his father's death at the age of seven. With the help of birds, Yared learned music and began to insert that into lyrics for the Ethiopian church. He arranged and composed many of the songs that are used today in the religious ceremonies that the Ethiopians chant and play still today. It was said that he wrote and composed numerous books of chants and songs for the church and became a favorite of the Ethiopian King, Gabra Masqal. After accidentally dropping his spear into Yared's foot, the king allowed him to have a request in forgiveness for his action. Yared asked to be allowed to live his life out in solitude in order to pray and compose for the rest of his life. His wish was lived out in the Simien Mountain range north of Gondar, Ethiopia *(ref. 21)*.

The Cross of Yared in the treasury on Tana Kirkos Island.

Aba Gabriel went on to explain that this particular cross was used by Yared until he died. After that it was brought to Tana Kirkos Island to be kept. Several years prior, there was a group from Europe who was given access to the island, in which during a diversion, someone hid the large cross in their clothing, and stole it away from the island. Gabriel was proud to show us the cross because it was located in the collection of a European man who had bought it on the open black market to add to his other artifacts. It was located and returned to Tana Kirkos in the ornate case that was made for it during its departure from the island. Aba Gabriel was obviously excited to show us, and even more thrilled to have it back on the island. It was beautiful, and a wonderful piece of Ethiopian history that has returned to its rightful place of holding.

THE CEREMONY AT THE ARK

After viewing and taking more photos of the small book of Jesus' meeting with His Father on Tana Kirkos, he closed up the historic animal skin pages, placed it on the shelf, and we walked out the door. He locked the various sets of locks, and we made our way to the archway. Again, removing our shoes, we walked past the ancient temple and onward to the platform of the footholds of the Ark. I knelt on the ground and cleared more debris that had gathered since our last journey there. I pulled a tape measure out and a small brush to clean the actual engravings into the stone. I measured the carvings once, and then did it again, just to make sure I wasn't getting this wrong. There was no doubt that the Ark rested here, and that His Son was given all of His knowledge, as in Isaiah's prophecy (7:14-16), and then confirmed in Luke (2:40) right here on this place. The evidence of the Ark was right in front of us, and the feeling that surrounds this place is simply undeniable.

I asked Gabriel if there was anything else written about the ceremonies that were held at this place, while the Ark was on Tana Kirkos. He said that there were other things written, including what the priest would do upon exciting the Holy of Holies. He stood with his horse-hair whip in his hand and began to demonstrate on the spot of the Ark, the dipping and sprinkling of blood on the Ark and the foot of the Ark on the rock slab, while swinging it eastward, just as described in Leviticus Chapter 14.

Top and bottom photos show Aba Gabriel and Jim discussing
the ancient ceremony on the Day of Atonement.

Then after covering the Throne of God (Mercy Seat) over,
he would then step from the Holy of Holies and look to the
East where he would see hundreds, if not thousands of papyrus
boats in the waters clearly below, with candles burning, waiting
for the announcement from the high priest, just as the priest
would do toward the people as seen in Numbers 2. I'm not sure
whether he even realized that his entire procession of instruction to us was laying perfectly alongside the Bible's description
of the events on the Day of Atonement. What an awe-inspiring
site that must have been to see those flickers of candlelight
across the waters as the people would gather. I told him that
it gave me goose-bumps just thinking about it. He turned his

head sideways and asked, "What is goose bimps?" I said, "No, goose-bumps," as I began to chuckle. I simply told him that it inspired me to think about such an event, rather than trying to explain what goose-bumps were.

I had brought with me a container with casting clay in it, and Gabriel was more than willing to allow me to make molds of the footholds of the Ark. We allowed them to set for a few minutes before we picked them up and laid them on a large leaf to carry with us while they dried. For now, we were finished in our work at this location, and we made our way back to the rocks in front of the treasury. Each of us grabbed a rock to sit upon, and we began to hold some more discussion about the events that had taken place here some two thousand years ago. The feeling that surrounds this place just overwhelms you. You can feel the presence of God, and it was like nothing I have felt before.

KING OF KINGS EMBEDDED IN STONE

Just when you think that you had seen enough, the puzzle continued to grow as Aba Gabriel said, "Let me take you up to the top of the cliff, I have something else to show you." We again took our shoes off, just after putting them back on when we left the platform of the Ark, and started to follow Gabriel up the steep cliff to a metal building under a massive tree, some sixty feet above Lake Tana's waters. He opened the door to the building to reveal an old bell that has been there for centuries. He then turned around as we followed him across the uneven slope of the narrow top of the wall. Far down to the left is the treasury building, backed by the jungle trees. To the right is a long, steep drop to the rocks, and waters of the lake. It was rough to walk in your bare feet across the rocks and at times we needed to stop to regain our sense about how high up we were. He proceeded to show us a covering over the area where Mary would have sat and prayed while Jesus was at the Holy of Holies with God upon the Mercy Seat. He said, "You like?" And I simply nodded to show him that it was amazing to see this. But then, he put his index finger up, indicating that he had one more thing to show me.

We turned around and began walking, and seemingly swaying, back down the slope atop the cliff. He stopped and cleared some leaves to show me an indention in the stone. I looked at it, but couldn't see what he was trying to show me. I was clueless on what he was trying to show me. He started to speak in his broken English, "Do you see the footprint?" I still wasn't seeing anything until I started clearing more of the dirt from the indention. All I can say is that I was completely blown away!

Aba Gabriel seen the enlargement of my eyes as I moved back a little. There was a set of footprints embedded in the solid rock. The left print was visible, but the right print, as I continued to clear smaller debris from the indention, was incredible. The only words I remembered uttering was, "Oh, wow!" Aba was just as astonished as I was as I pulled my brush out and kept sweeping dirt from the impression in the stone.

Before I go any further, let me explain this from the beginning. Jim and Penny Caldwell made significant finds during their research in the area around Jebel al-Lawz (believed to be the real location of Mt. Sinai) in Saudi Arabia, and especially with their finds near the split rock of Moses *(ref. 2)*. Their finds involved a series of rocks throughout the valley in which sandals and feet are carved into the stone claiming the land for themselves, as seen in Deuteronomy 11:24a:

> *Every place whereon the soles of your feet shall*
> *tread shall be yours...* (Deuteronomy 11:24a)

The Israelites were simply to claim their land by carving, or tracing their feet into the stones as somewhat of a marker of ownership. But these were simply the carved prints, not embedded footprints.

Although this footprint was a complete surprise, it's one that I will continue to research along with other reports that I have heard of footprints along the path from Egypt to Ethiopia, and back into Israel. As I process all of this, I will continue to be the tool that God guides me to research further. I will never dismiss even the most impossible knowing that all things are possible with God. And that has proved more true than ever with these discoveries.

I stood there, high atop this cliff, with tears rolling down my face, knowing that there was much more to research to come. Jesus had now been given all that He was to know and do for mankind in order to redeem it. The purpose had been completed. You can't help but think that he climbed to the top of this rock wall and embedded His mark into the stone as to say, "It has been completed." A stamp of finality, if you would. That kept running through my mind. It was an act of completion...I'm in awe at the power He had in order to do this.

This was all part of another revelation that God was laying out. Just as we stood there on the cliff, large white and black eagles began to screech loudly in the tree next to us. The friendship and trust that was building on this island was amazing. They freely allow me to work, research, read manuscripts, and document all of this without hesitation. I have watched this trust build both ways over the years, and now I believe that all God is trying to show me is really part of a huge picture to bring reality to His Word in a whole different way to a world that has lost its trust in anything.

Until I could return again to continue the research on this project, I convinced them to allow me to pay to have an iron covering with a lid to be built over these prints to protect them from weathering. I knew I'd be back again soon, because I knew there would be a great deal of evidence that would need to be accumulated in order to build a case for these footprint indentions. If it was God who revealed them to me, then I know it will be God who will take it to the next level.

Chapter 10:

THE GUARDIAN GRAVEYARD

TIME AFTER TIME, WHENEVER I've thought that I've seen it all, something else has been revealed during this incredible journey into this biblical land of hidden secrets. There was no exception to that theory on one particular Tuesday morning in April of 2014. At around three in the morning, my phone began to ring with a very unusual sound to it. Your first reaction at a call that early is to jump and grab the phone in fear. But, before I could find it on my nightstand, I noticed that the ring was that of a call coming from Ethiopia. With their time seven hours ahead of the U.S. Eastern Time Zone, to them it was mid-morning, and they had been up and about for several hours. I struggled to hit the right buttons because the bright glare of the phone was nearly blinding my newly awakened eyes. I was taken back, somewhat, after I said, "hello", when, on the other end, Aba Gabriel said, "Hello, Mr. Jim, Hello?" Somehow, with his Ethiopian cell phone, Aba had gone up to the high point on the island of Tana Kirkos to get a signal to call me. What really caught me off guard was his urgency to his voice. I told him to hold on a minute as I climbed out of bed, to make my way out into the hallway. I turned to Sherri before leaving the room to encourage her that it was Aba Gabriel, and that everything was alright.

He began to speak quickly, and with the broken English moving even faster, I couldn't make out a word he was saying. I had to ask him to slow down and speak in a more-calm manner so I could understand what he was saying. He began to insist that I come back to Ethiopia immediately. We had just been there for most of February, but he wanted me back there right away. I asked him, "What is wrong?" He replied quickly, "I need you to come. We found things in the ground. Bodies, Mr. Jim. You must come quickly!" "Bodies?" I asked. I guess my curiosity had peaked, and honestly, I was a little confused. He answered me, "Yes, bodies in the ground when we were digging. Please come, thank you." I told him that I would try to get there in about three weeks and he simply said, "Ishy, ishy," or "O.K., O.K." in English. And then it seemed, just as quickly as the call came in, and he began to speak, the call was now over and he simply hung up on his end. It's three in the morning, I was just awakened from a great sleep, and I'm told there are bodies on Tana Kirkos, and then nothing! This is my life. One mystery to the next, but I had to chuckle. I was totally lost on this one. The only thing I knew, we had built up such a great friendship that I trusted him in knowing that he wouldn't have called if he didn't truly need me.

Within three weeks, I was on a plane and again on our way to Ethiopia in order to grab the first flight we could get to Bahir

Dar. Misgana and I did catch a flight to Bahir Dar, but when we finally arrived, it was much too late to get a boat to Tana Kirkos that day. Besides, the almost thirteen-hour flight to Ethiopia, and then another hour to Bahir Dar, had taken its toll on me and I was totally worn out. We grabbed some dinner, found our beds, and made it an early night.

As always, Misgana was right on time to meet me for an early breakfast as the sun was still below the horizon to the east. You could already see the silhouettes of Tankwa fishing boats taking their place on the lake, and kingfishers were hovering the waters, making quick dives for a morning catch. The boat arrived at the dock, and I boarded with Misgana leading the way. The captain shoved off, and we were on our way again. The water this particular morning had a little wave to it, but it was the misty splash that made it particularly cool with a slight fog lying low on the waters. The breeze was cool and my eyes began to water, so I had to get my sunglasses on early. We pulled up next to a fisherman in a Tankwa to see his boat filled with fish already. I knew there would be much to do on this journey, as we were still to travel to Axum, and some other work still to do when we get back to Addis Ababa. But, I also knew that the Lord had something for us to do here first. It seemed like the puzzle was growing larger upon each journey to this beautiful, but mysterious country. That puzzle grew a little larger with this trip, but we knew the pieces to fill it in would be soon to follow with each new open door.

Three hours had gone by fairly quickly, as we could see Tana Kirkos Island off in the distance. As we pulled up to the island's base, we came to an abrupt halt, ramming the outer rocks hard. The captain of the boat threw a rope to the monks waiting on the jagged rocks that were protruding out from the water. The captain backed the boat up and took one more move toward the island, and again we hit the unseen rocks under the waters. The monks held onto the rope tightly, as I stepped to the edge of the boat and took a leap to the rocks on the island. As I hit, one of the rocks dislodged, but quickly a monk grabbed my arm and held me long enough so I could get my balance onto another rock. We then made our way up the slick rocky cliff to the top of the island plateau above.

It seems like you never know what you're going to run into when you're in these far-away lands. As we arrived at the top of the cliff we heard some rustling around near in the trees near a small little shed to the left of the rocks. As we moved closer, we realized that it wasn't a monk trying to get up, but a very large Nile monitor lizard hissing and warning us of his territory. Then, without warning, the monitor whipped its large tail and scurried quickly to the rocky edge, took one leap, and dropped some sixty feet into the waters below. Without any doubt, it got the heart rate up, because we didn't even have time to react. But it was another encounter of many along our journeys that adds to the overall experience of the surroundings.

Just after we turned around, Aba Gabriel was standing waiting for us with a smile on his face. As always, he warmly greeted me with a hard, embracing hug of mutual respect. It is such an honor to me that our friendship has been so richly blessed, and we have built the relationship with trust over the years. I am very thankful for that. After his welcome, he began to lead us through the jungle, walking past the coffee trees, the vegetables that were growing in the clearing, and the papaya trees that were filled with fruit. As we arrived behind the old stone treasury, we made a left to the side of the building, and things were very different than the last time we were there. To the south, to the right of the treasury, there was now a large hole in the ground. They had begun to dig a footer to pray over to possibly build a new treasury. As they dug, they realized they had found more than they were planning on, and continued to dig. Now, they had a hole approximately five feet deep, twenty-five-feet long, and twelve feet wide. However, their digging was halted when they uncovered a highly unusual slab of stone. Not realizing their discovery, they broke up the stone and stacked it along with other rocks in a fence row. As I glanced at them, I quickly discovered that these stones were grooved tops to ancient tombs. The top pieces had an outer groove, while the bottom part of the tomb had a matching inner groove to hold them together. It was very similar to the Egyptian style, or even the look of modern day vault. I picked up the broken top and bottom pieces and showed Aba how it worked, and he simply nodded, and then motioned for me to follow him into the hole.

As I descended into the large hole in the ground, I couldn't help but think to myself, "Who were these stone coffins built for? Who could this possibly be on such a significant guarded island like Tana Kirkos?" You have to put this island into perspective, it was the place of the Ark of the Covenant, the Throne of God, and the host to a summit meeting of heavenly proportions. After getting five or six steps into the hole, I couldn't believe what sat in front of me. My eyes must have grown to the size of saucers. Right before me was a body, or should I say the skeletal remains of an ancient human lying in the dirt before me. I walked over, knelt down, and just gazed at this find. We cautiously continued to dig, with Aba Gabriel, and Misgana right at my side. There were numerous femurs and pelvic bones of a people who were obviously small in stature.

As I walked around in the gap in the ground, I saw what appeared to be a skull slightly protruding from the edge of the dirt. Unfortunately, most of these bodies were brittle and had been eaten by termites, but a few were retrievable. I sat my backpack on the ground and began to pull my brushes and tools from it. Aba had grabbed a shallow bucket for the remains to be put into. Although he felt that there was no need to preserve the remains, he still felt that anything that was removed must stay nearby close to the burial site. For me, it was a different story. I began to slowly brush the dirt around the skull and was able to safely retract most of the cranial portion from the hardened dirt. The rest of the skull had disintegrated. As I continued to brush, I was able to remove a full jawbone and a full set of teeth from this particular man of the ancient past. There was body after body seemingly laid out in a pattern. Most were lying with their arms upward or crossed, and a few held silver or bronze crosses within their grasps. Interestingly, they were all facing the East, which agrees with biblical texts. There were nearly a dozen bodies in that particular burial ground from the ancient times that the Guardians of today knew nothing about.

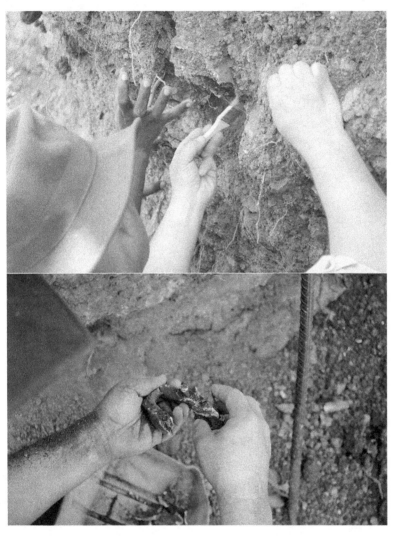

Top: Excavating a skull from the Guardian Graveyard. Bottom: Ancient Guardian of the Ark Jawbone excavated from the gravesite.

Top: Jim and Misgana looking into a tomb.
Bottom: Jim showing the top of a broken tomb covering.

This all took me back to the very first visit to Tana Kirkos Island, when the leader of the expedition at that time brought the shovel along with him to dig for what he thought, was a Knight's Templar remains under the engraved stone cross on the rock wall. He had a theory that a Templar was buried in this place, and after a discussion with the Aba Gabriel, there was no way that the island's guardian was going to allow him to dig upon that holy ground. I can remember very vividly, I knew that Aba's request not to dig on that day was through a long tradition passed down through the ages, and I felt for him. That's when I stepped in to say that this was holy ground to them, and it would be a dishonor to dig around this spot. We all thought it was because of them knowing the Ark was brought here. Little did any of us know at the time, including Aba Gabriel, that the stone cross on the wall was not only marking holy ground, but it was marking the ancient burial ground of the guardian priests of Tana Kirkos Island from centuries ago.

As Aba and my relationship began to grow, I truly believe that it all began at this place of the cross that really set this friendship in gear. God had brought us here, both of us, and God is responsible for all that has taken place.

Chapter 11:

THE DAY THE EARTH SHOOK

WHAT A DAY IT had to be. Jesus had been tried, scourged, spit upon, mocked, and it was time to make the long walk, with a cross upon His shoulders, to a place called Golgotha. The man was in pain but the God within knew this had to be done. The walk begins as Jesus' blood dripped upon the streets of Jerusalem, and He struggled with every step to stay on His feet. As He dragged the cross, He fell to the ground in horrible pain, and this strength had left Him. A soldier grabbed a watcher from the crowd, an African man from Cyrene in Libya to help take up the cross with Him. As Simon, the Libyan, took the bulk of the weight of the cross upon his shoulders, Jesus stayed in tow, knowing He couldn't let go in order to fulfill the covenant to redeem God's creation of man through His Salvation and return.

> *And he bearing his cross went forth into a place*
> *called the place of a skull, which is called in*
> *the Hebrew Golgotha: Where they crucified him,*
> *and two other with him, on either side one, and*
> *Jesus in the midst.* (John 19:17-18)

The Messiah had now been placed upon the cross, and was gasping for each and every breath, as He looked below to see His mother, Mary, others who followed Him, and His disciple John. To the left and right were thieves, and the mockers continued their rant. Yes, the same two, Titus and Dumachus, Jesus encountered as a small child in Egypt that He foretold would be at His sides on the cross that we discussed in chapter 4. But things were beginning to change as His time on the cross lingered. Darkness had fallen across the land during the midday, and after Jesus called out that He was thirsty, He then cried out...

> *It is finished: and he bowed his head, and gave*
> *up the ghost.* (John 19:30)

From here the chaos truly began for the world that was witnessing the beginning of the resurrection of the Savior of the world. While His blood was still freshly flowing off the bottom of His toes, and continuing to the ground, Jesus the Christ had just completed the first part of His work on this Earth, but it was just the beginning of what would turn out to be an unforgettable event upon the land of the Bible.

THE TEMPLE VEIL

At this point you can only imagine the fear as the priests in the temple were second guessing their actions in pursuing the crucifixion of Jesus. As He hung upon the cross and gasped for each breath, they had to be thinking, "What have we done?"

His cries from the cross were not that of a man that was dying, but from a Messiah that was preparing. He cried out for mercy upon the people, and you can't help but feel the trembling of the high priest as he made his way back to the temple, not willing to see the final results of this One who claimed to be God in the flesh push Himself upward to grab a breath to resist suffocation before His final words were spoken. These Jewish priests had denied the One who would give His life for them and the rest of mankind, but their selfishness and pride would not let them admit to knowing, or recognizing that the Son of God was hanging from a cross back on Calvary's hill. But without any doubt, the moment that Jesus knew it all had been accomplished and cried out, "*It is finished*," they surely felt the power of the beginning of the Messiah's Words.

At the point that Jesus had accomplished it all and gave up the ghost on the cross, a series of events of historic and heavenly nature began to take place. First was the damage to the temple's veil that separated all people from God's law:

*And the veil of the temple was rent in twain from
the top to the bottom.* (Mark 15:38)

And in Matthew:

*And, behold, the veil of the temple was
rent in twain from the top to the bottom;*
(Matthew 27:51a)

The significance of this event is overwhelming. The thick temple veil that separated God's people from the Holy of Holies, or His law which was now accomplished through Jesus when He gave up the ghost, was shredded not by someone below, but by God from the top to the bottom. Surely from this point the priests knew that they had been a part of a murder, but also the fear of their role of putting the Son of God to death.

But that wasn't all. We learn that in Matthew 27:51b, that the earth began to quake and the rocks began to fall and break:

> *...and the earth did quake, and the rocks rent;*
> (Matthew 27:51b)

We can only assume that some of the rocks that the Bible refers to here are the pillars and walls made of stone, not only in the temple, but from the mountains, the walls of the city, and beyond. But that wasn't all. More profound events were witnessed including the bodies of the saints rising from the graves and going into the city:

> *And the graves were opened; and many bodies of the saints which slept arose, And came out of the graves after his resurrection, and went into the holy city, and appeared unto many.*
> (Matthew 27:52-53)

And then the first salvation through faith by God's grace after the resurrection takes place by one of the most unlikely, a Roman centurion:

> *Now when the centurion, and they that were with him, watching Jesus, saw the earthquake, and those things that were done, they feared greatly, saying, Truly this was the Son of God.* (Matthew 27:52-54)

Think about this: the sky had turned dark at noon during Jesus' time on the cross and stayed that way until around three in the afternoon when Jesus said, *it is finished*:

> *and there was a darkness over all the earth until the ninth hour. And the sun was darkened,* (Luke 23:44b-45a)

> *there was darkness over the whole land until the ninth hour.* (Mark 15:33b)

> *Now from the sixth hour there was darkness over all the land unto the ninth hour.* (Matthew 27:45)

You can't help but think of the fear on the people when the skies over Jerusalem, and possibly across the Earth went dark in the middle of the day. Then this man claiming to be the Son of God cried out that "*It was finished,*" at that moment the Earth began to shake, the temple veil ripped from top to bottom opening the Holy of Holies to mankind to have direct relationship with God, and the rocks began to break apart in hills, the fields, and even the buildings throughout the land. It did not say that only Jerusalem began to shake, but the entire Earth shook from this great quake. Everyone, including those that knew Him best, had to be in fear of what was happening when the One they had trusted had just cried out, died, and the appearance of chaos began to ensue. This, as we know, was the beginning of the fulfillment of the cleansing of those who believed and will believe through the blood of Christ. But the real question now comes, what else took place on this unforgettable day?

THE DAY THE EARTH SHOOK

So why talk about the day of the crucifixion of Christ? Let me explain. In February of 2016 our team planned a return trip to Ethiopia. After our arrival in the capital city of Addis Ababa, we made our way to various locations across the country including work in Axum, a quick visit to Gondar, and then the long drive through the valleys, mountains, and across the various terrains, in order to make our way to Bahir Dar on the shores of Lake Tana. Our team, consisting of twelve, took a bumpy drive out to visit the beauty of the Blue Nile Falls, and then to our motel for an evening dinner and then a night time devotion, followed by a teaching session I conducted about what took place on this lake and the surrounding area. We then said our goodnights, and Sherri and I were off to attempt to take in a good night's sleep.

For one of the few times during this trip I did get a fairly decent sleep. We were up early and made our way out to break-fast. By the time everyone had arrived and eaten, the boat had arrived, and we were off in the early morning sunrise across the calm waters of Lake Tana. Tankwa boats were abundant with fishermen taking in their catches, and close behind were pel-icans hoping for the kindness of the men in the boat. I pulled everyone together and gave them more of the history of the islands on the lake, and then we participated in the Lord's supper and went into prayer. The team then found a place of comfort on the boat to take in the sights and the beautiful views that were before them.

Three hours later our journey across the placidness of the massive lake had brought our arrival to Tana Kirkos again. It seemed as though so much had centered here, and all of our contacts in the country had always pointed us back to the island of mystery over and over again. This time was more of a research and review for many of our group, and a time of devo-tion for the ladies, since they weren't able to go where the men were trekking into the holy places of the island.

After making our way up the cliff to the top of the island and trekking through the jungle, we arrived at the old stone trea-sury building facing the high cliff wall in front, jungle on the two sides, and a view of the old temple to the south. Misgana went ahead to locate Aba Gabriel, but he was nowhere to be found. Little did we know, he was back where the ladies were as he greeted Sherri, along with Bev Regehr, Kathryn Pearce, and others. That is one great way to know that our friendship has grown as he came to them first before making his way to us on the other side of the jungle. Moments later, he came with a smile on his face, and we embraced to honor our friendship that has been evident in its growth since my first visit nearly seven years prior. We shared a few words with each other, and I was amazed at the English that he had learned since the last time we had seen each other. He followed in shaking the hands with Tim Moore, and others that traveled with us, as I introduced each that were new.

After we shared with each other a little more, Aba Gabriel walked us by the hole in the ground where we excavated the guardian priests a couple of years earlier (as we discussed in the previous chapter). We walked in front of the old treasury building, and we stopped there as Aba went into his quarters next to it. He emerged with a few sprigs of an olive tree that he wanted to show me that he was growing from his visit to Jerusalem's Garden of Gethsemane. We then made our way back around the hole to the rock fence that surrounds the old temple where during many of my previous travels to the island you could hear the sounds bellowing out of the large hollowed out wooden drums covered with stretched animal hide. But today the sounds were silent, except for the two large fish eagles screeching from above.

Finally, we had arrived at the place of the Ark's footholds as I turned to the men to remove their shoes from this point. Just as I had done many times before since my discovery of the footholds, I walked to place of the Ark and went to my knees where I had collapsed so many years earlier. I have such a peace at this place and really, it's like I don't realize that anyone else is around me while I'm on that spot. Aba came over and sat beside me, as he could tell that I was in prayer. I turned to the men and explained the area to them, and then they followed me up to the site where the Ark was lifted up from the waters some sixty foot below, upon its arrival centuries before. I then showed them the final resting place of the Levite High Priest that had brought the Ark there, and then showed them the pole holes that had been discovered some years prior to my first arrival there. I showed them the stone bowl that the priest would dip the blood sacrifice in for sprinkling on the Ark, as Aba Gabriel began to demonstrate with his horse-hair whip.

Two of the rounded top, "V" shaped pole holes to hold up the Holy of Holies that broke off the platform on Tana Kirkos Island.

Each of the men had the opportunity to go to the place and pray on the spot where Jesus sat with His Father during God's appearance on the Mercy Seat while training His Son. I knew others wanted to spend more time there, but I had some questions that had been tugging at me for a few years now. For several years, Sherri had been urging me to ask Aba Gabriel about the day that Jesus died on the cross. You have to remember, the Ark of the Covenant, with the Mercy Seat atop, was sitting on this spot in Ethiopia on the day that Christ was nailed in sacrifice on the cross in Israel. It sat in a makeshift Holy of Holies, and Sherri had asked me over and over again to pose the question to Aba, "What happened the day Jesus went to the cross and gave up the ghost?"

Now, a few minutes earlier, before we left the ladies on the other side of the island, Sherri leaned over to the side of my face and said, "Jim, don't forget to ask him." I knew exactly what she was talking about and I nodded my head. Now, sitting on the place of the footholds, I didn't want to let this opportunity pass from my mind again. You see, there has been something about this place that I could never explain. During my discovery of the footholds, there were seven indentions carved into the stone. What I could never explain was that the three center holes were about three and half inches off-center to the north than the other four indentions on the corners. Each time I have come here, there has been a purpose of research, measurements, and then reflection. But this time I needed to be focused. I looked up to Aba Gabriel, as he made his way down to his knees in front of me. Slowly I said to him, in order to make sure he understood what I was asking, "Sherri has been asking me for years about the day that Jesus died upon the cross. She has felt the Spirit lead her to ask, what happened on this island at the moment in time when He died?"

At this point I saw a calmness of true trust come over his face. It was like he had just felt a confidence in me that God was leading me to ask the questions that he had been waiting for me to ask. I didn't want to let Sherri down, and it seemed as though Aba had been waiting for this question for years, and now here it was. It also seemed as though his English was plain as he explained, "When Jesus died on the cross (demonstrating with his arms out to the side), the Earth shook. The temple (motioning but not having the words for veil and making the sound of a tear from top to bottom)." I nodded as he went on, "The Earth shakes all over, all the earth, as it did right here." My mouth came open, as the other men felt the presence of God as the rest of the revelation from Aba Gabriel continued, "When the Earth shake, the pole holes (pointing at the broken off pole holes in the little metal building), break off and fall off the rock.

Two black arrows show center cracks from the earthquake, white arrow shows where two pole holes broke from. Note small covering to far right is another in-tact pole hole.

(Then pointing to three off-center holes), they moved (motioning with his hands towards me on the ground)." Aba dropped back down to his knees in front of me and started to show me the large cracks in the rock on both sides of the middle footholds on the rock slab platform. It was just simply amazing. On both sides of the center holes were cracks that took place at the moment Jesus said "It is finished," and the Earth shook. It was the same time that the temple veil ripped from top to bottom, and the same time the rocks broke apart as described in Matthew 27:51. I had tried to explain this to myself so many times before on why they were offset. I remember once a few years ago, Dave Kochis even asked me, after looking at a photo of the plat-

form, why they looked offset. Now I had an answer to his question. I pulled out my tape measure again and started to do some calculations of the footholds again. All three center footholds measure three and a half inches off-center.

In the center of the entire remaining platform was a massive crack showing the power of the quake

Top: Jim measuring Ark's footholds.
Bottom: Measuring to show one of the three center footholds three and half inch shift from the earthquake.

when it occurred on the day of Christ on the cross. I needed to get a little more confirmation on this, so I asked the Aba how he knew of this event happening on the island with the Ark of the Covenant on the day Jesus was on the cross. He responded, "It is written. Come, I will show you." He then led me back to the old treasury building and proceeded to show me the writings documenting the account of the that day in an ancient text written on animal hide and stored within the archives of this treasure trove of manuscripts. With Sherri's question for me to ask Aba Gabriel being fully revealed, now so many years later, the answer was obvious. And the evidence on the site is overwhelming. Think about it, the Holy of Holies over the throne of God simply collapsed on that prophetic day right there on this small island on Lake Tana, Ethiopia.

Aba went on to show me that the entire platform was much bigger before this event. It was like a big relief that had just been lifted off of him. For the others, you could see the amazement on their faces. Tim simply shook his head, as to say, "Just incredible." To the others, I believe they simply got it, and began to see that this was truly a special place in the eyes of the Lord. The power of the entire event that happened the day the Earth shook was beyond measure. Think about this again, the day Jesus dies upon the cross, the whole planet shook. On Tana Kirkos, the throne of God was sitting in a makeshift Holy of Holies. The cliff broke apart and two of the pole holes broke from the ledge and into the waters below. The platform that the Ark of the Covenant and the Throne of God was sitting upon cracked and shifted, as the Ark bounced on the stone while it shook, collapsing the Holy of Holies tent down upon it. This is somewhat symbolic in a way referencing that the Ark was to be covered. If the tent simply fell over, the Ark would have been exposed, but God covered His throne from the view of the people in a dramatic fashion.

Even though Sherri had never been allowed to go to the place of the Ark, the Lord lead her to know that something happened here on that day when Jesus gave the ultimate sacrifice upon the cross. If the throne was here, and the power of the Ark of the Covenant has always been known to be the Holy Spirit which was sent out from within, then the perfect picture that only God could paint had just been completed. Or should I say, it had just begun!

Chapter 12:

THE QUESTION: WHY ETHIOPIA?

FROM THE BEGINNING OF the Creation, God has entrusted this land of Ethiopia enough to include it over 50 times in His Word. He had favored this land since the beginning of Creation, through the holy summit on His Throne and His Son's fulfillment there, to the times of when God in the flesh gave up the ghost on the cross. You can't help but know that He will use this land one more time in the future. It had always been said that Adam's remains had to come to the cross of Jesus to fulfill the covenant between the first Adam and the last Adam (Jesus), but little did all of us know that God had a perfect plan in place to protect the secrets of the Bible, in a land that no one would look to, until the time that it will be needed again.

Many people have offered opinions about the importance of Ethiopia to biblical history. There is no denying that Ethiopia is one of the most mentioned countries throughout the Scriptures. They play enough importance that God included them in key Scriptures and some of the most important roles in history, both in the past and in the future. From the Garden of Eden, to Moses' wife Zipporah, to Solomon's attraction, to the return of the Ark of the Covenant, to the reasons why Luke spent so much time on the Ethiopians in Acts chapter eight, Ethiopia's masterful role in history proves unquestionable. One thing is for sure, this African country may hold more than the secrets of Jesus' past–it may also hold the keys to Jesus' future reign.

RIVER NEAR EDEN

One of the most interesting Scriptures in the early texts of the Bible came with the foundation of the earth in Genesis:

> *And a river went out of Eden to water the garden; and from thence it was parted, and became into four heads...And the name of the second river is Gihon: the same is it that compasseth the whole land of Ethiopia.* (Genesis 2:10, 13)

This particular Scripture has generated much controversy about the exact location of the Garden of Eden. Evidently, Ethiopia was greatly treasured by God to include them in the opening pages of His Holy Word.

MOSES' ETHIOPIAN WIFE

Another clear clue to the importance of Ethiopia in the Scriptures comes with the marriage of Moses to an Ethiopian woman of color:

> *And Miriam and Aaron spake against Moses because of the Ethiopian woman whom he had married: for he had married an Ethiopian woman.* (Numbers 12:1)

We see in this Scripture the disagreement about Moses' marriage to a dark-skinned woman, possibly named Zipporah (Exodus 2:21). Because of this disagreement between Moses and his siblings, Miriam (who appears to be the instigator since she is mentioned first) and Aaron, God cursed Miriam with leprosy to show His anger upon her apparent racial judgment. Of course, after much crying out in prayer by Moses, Miriam was healed of her curse.

What was the real reason why we were brought to the knowledge of Moses' wife? Could this mention in Numbers be our introduction to possibly foretelling of the resting place of the Ark of the Covenant to be guarded by the Ethiopians until the time it is to be returned to Jerusalem? Could it also be a telling account that this is where Jesus would travel, in order to meet with His Father for just over three months to gain the knowledge and blessings for His future? To me it is interesting that God would have chosen certain passages to be included in Bible text if they didn't have a further meaning. We have to assume that the passages mentioned here were to give us a closer look into the future reference to Ethiopia, and its importance to the times to come, referring to the Mercy Seat, the Ark of the Covenant, and the protectors of these artifacts. Everything included in the Holy Word of God has an importance in the past, present and the future. Again, this appears to have a more intricate role than we may have first thought.

THE PROPHETIC SCRIPTURES OF ISAIAH

Even though there are many other Scriptures that precede Isaiah 18 that mention Ethiopia, this is one of the most prophetic Scriptures that alludes to the whereabouts of the Ark of the Covenant's current location and future events leading up to the Ark's return to Jerusalem. During our first journey, before my discovery of the footholds and the ancient book on the cliffside overlooking Axum, Ethiopia during a cool evening, Bob Cornuke and I were relaxing in our chairs next to small fire that one of the motel workers had started for us after our long day of work in a makeshift clinic and exploration of the tombs of the kings. Even though I was wearing a jacket because the warm days had turned to star studded cool nights, I can remember that I couldn't wait to pop open an ice-cold Coke to splash some taste of home on my palate and wash down that gritty taste of dust and sand. As Bob and I sat talking about the next day's adventures, he asked if I had read his book Relic Quest. I told him that I honestly had only read the parts that had nothing to do with the Ark of the Covenant because I didn't want a pre-conceived bias about my purpose on this exploration. He then asked, "Have you read Isaiah 18 yet?" Without any hesitation, I told him that I had read Isaiah many times before, and I considered it one of my favorite and most intriguing books of the Bible. He nodded his head and the conversation shifted as Dave Kochis and Craig Newmaker pulled up chairs alongside of us.

This topic never came up again until our team sat on bench seats in Barhir Dar one evening for a Bible study just two hundred yards from the shore line of Lake Tana. Beneath the lobby canopy of the motel, which looked much like a thatched hut roof with no doors and an open entry right to the front desk, the team gathered to listen to Bob's explanation about the strong possibility that the Ark could still be in Ethiopia today. While there, I had a flurry of thoughts, ideas, and revelations spinning in my head. Pieces of our journey that had already taken place, and pieces impressed upon me started to make sense, and it all began to fall into place.

Even though this story is not about the Ark of the Covenant specifically, its appearance is crucial as the place where God came to meet with His Son. The finding of the footholds of the Ark was a huge piece of the puzzle; with this evidence as truth, we must be able to place the Ark somewhat in this region of the country for this particular encounter. During the study of Isaiah 18, it was like all of the events beginning in the middle of the night in Gatlinburg, Tennessee to kneeling in front of the trumpets in Axum had now become a bright shining light of reality to me. It was like a look into the future, to a real time and place, unveiling before my eyes. As my thoughts began to wander, I hurriedly scratched notes and flipped open to other passages where I had made notes along this journey. Isaiah 18 elevated this entire journey from an "everybody has their own thoughts" to "Oh, my goodness, have we just walked on Holy ground" reality. Let's look at this Scripture closely:

> *"Woe to the land shadowing with wings, which is beyond the rivers of Ethiopia: That sendeth ambassadors by the sea, even in vessels of bulrushes upon the waters, saying, Go, ye swift messengers, to a nation scattered and peeled, to a people terrible from their beginning hitherto; a nation meted out and trodden down, whose land the rivers have spoiled! All ye inhabitants of the world, and dwellers on the earth, see ye, when he lifteth up an ensign on the mountains; and when he bloweth a trumpet, hear ye. In that time, shall the present be brought unto the LORD of hosts of a people scattered and peeled, and from a people terrible from their beginning hitherto; a nation meted out and trodden under foot, whose land the rivers have spoiled, to the place of the name of the LORD of hosts, the mount Zion,"* (Isaiah 18:1-3, 7)

Breaking this down more closely, we see in verse one that the thoughts on this passage describe Ethiopia as it is now, not necessarily as it was when Isaiah wrote this Scripture. Remember, he was a prophet and was talking about a future time, not the current time he lived in. Some say the *shadowing with wings* (or in some translations of *buzzing wings*) could be the flies or mosquitos buzzing around. The KJV *shadowing with wings*, or closer to the Hebrew translation of *covered in wings*, most likely is referring to the beautiful eagles that soar through the skies over the region. It's followed by a passage pin-pointing the region, *beyond the rivers of Ethiopia,* which flow greatly in the northern mountain regions of this country. It goes on to tell us about ambassadors who will be traveling in the reed, bulrush, or papyrus boats that the fishermen of Lake Tana still travel in today.

Tankwa (papyrus reed boat) fisherman paddling in before storms move over Lake Tana.

212

The Scripture continues to describe the people of Ethiopia, and how their nation has been somewhat sacrificed in order to protect something of great significance and value. This includes the disease and even the spoiled waters that they are plagued with today. When it describes to us, *a people terrible from their beginning hitherto*, I found in a study at the Hebrew Union College in Cincinnati that this reference is speaking of people who knew sin from the beginning, which brings us back to the knowledge that they have been here since God's Creation. But then it turns to a time when there will be a blast of the trumpets from the mountains of Ethiopia. The northern region of Ethiopia contains many mountain regions including the Simien Mountains and the Adwa Mountains as two of the most identified. This all makes you wonder if the trumpets could once again be those housed today in the treasury of the Ark in Axum. These trumpets, the trumpets of Moses, were blown to call the people to the tabernacle for instruction (Numbers 10:1), as well as for the announcement of the Ark's arrival when it was moved from place to place;

> *And David danced before the LORD with all*
> *his might; and David was girded with a linen*
> *ephod. So, David and all the house of Israel*
> *brought up the ark of the LORD with shouting,*
> *and with the sound of the trumpet. And as the*
> *ark of the LORD came into the city of David...*
> (2 Samuel 6:14-16)

Finally, a sign will be brought forth in those mountains, and as verse seven shares, a singular present, or gift of holy high nature, will be brought from Ethiopia to Jesus in Jerusalem, and it will be taken to Him in what it describes as the place where the Lord will rule from in the Holy of Holies in the third temple. When I re-examined this Scripture, it stopped me cold. In my continued study, I found that I had incorrectly interpreted it as meaning the "present time" instead of a present, or gift, brought in an appointed time period. In-depth study shows that *"the present"* will be something of great value to Christ and it will be revealed from the mountains of Ethiopia, and will go to Him in the *place of the name of the LORD of hosts, the mount Zion,* in which we know from many other Scriptures is the Holy of Holies, where Jesus will take up His throne in Jerusalem. With even closer review of Scriptures, we know that the Mercy Seat, the solid gold covering of the Ark of the Covenant, was actually the Throne of God's appearance on this earth as He would *dwell between the two cherubim.* One could speculate through the many Scriptures that support the fact, that this same Mercy Seat will one day return to Christ as His throne, and He will reign from that same place as His Father did.

Without any doubt, this Scripture is a compelling glance into a future event with Isaiah pin-pointing Ethiopia as we know it. This is not the Ethiopia with a building empire found during that particular time in history. To set up the Ark's movement from Jerusalem, during our study he shared that at the same time as the evil King Manasseh's reign and defilement of the first temple, another temple matching that of Solomon's dimensions had been built in Aswan, Egypt on the Nile River on the island of Elephantine. This southern Egyptian location can be confirmed through many Levitical papyri and scrolls left at the site. And with an incredible view of the Ark's presence with the Egyptian Pharaoh Necho in 2 Chronicles 35 taking his orders to march into battle directly from God Himself, we have great evidence that the Ark was located in Egypt. With a pagan god-driven nation now getting its orders from the one true God, we can assume the faith of this particular pharaoh had changed.

Continuing to look further, we see the Levites, according to historical records, simply left the site of the Elephantine Island temple and moved on to somewhere else. It was within a few years that the Ark's arrival was reported on the island of Tana Kirkos, which would have been a straight journey to the south down to the Nile to the Blue Nile, and into Lake Tana, its feeding point. From here, the Ark rested on this island in a makeshift tabernacle for centuries, until King Ezana claimed it for his kingdom in Axum. The most amazing aspect of these claims is the overwhelming evidence that backs each step of this journey. This is a journey that many have overlooked or dismissed over the years. One reason I believe it is overlooked is the power of tradition to shy away from anything that may be new information that could challenge what man has decided is truth, and not what God has shown us as proof.

THE CONTROVERSY OF JEREMIAH

After I had begun the speaking circuit following my journeys into Ethiopia, the biggest question that always came up
was the use of Jeremiah 3:16 as the Scripture that was to prove
that we don't need the Ark of the Covenant, and that it is gone
forever. I loved it every time I would hear folks discussing this
Scripture before I ever took the podium. Once again, and rightfully so, with the standard tradition, we see what appears to be
a prophecy of Jeremiah exclaiming that the Ark is no longer
needed in history:

> *And it shall come to pass, when ye be multiplied*
> *and increased in the land, in those days, saith*
> *the LORD, they shall say no more, The ark of*
> *the covenant of the LORD: neither shall it come*
> *to mind: neither shall they remember it; neither*
> *shall they visit it; neither shall that be done any*
> *more.* (Jeremiah 3:16)

This verse does tell us that there really won't be any need
for the Ark in history again. It has served its purpose as Jesus
came to us in order to become the Ark while holding the Law
of God within Him. What many traditionalists don't do is read
on to verse seventeen which gives the rest of the story:

> *At that time they shall call Jerusalem the*
> *throne of the LORD; and all the nations shall*

be gathered unto it, to the name of the LORD,
to Jerusalem: neither shall they walk any
more after the imagination of their evil heart.
(Jeremiah 3:17)

Completing the story, we see a period of time will pass once again. It appears as though this is the same time period that Isaiah mentioned in verse seven of chapter eighteen proclaiming that there will be a specified time period that Christ will take up His throne in Jerusalem in the Holy of Holies in the Temple. Again, we can gather from numerous other biblical texts that the mentioned throne will be the Mercy Seat which rests above the Ark of the Covenant. As the Ark itself will no longer be needed, we also see that the separate covering of gold, the Mercy Seat, will play a most intricate role upon the return of Christ.

EZEKIEL'S LOOK INTO THE THRONE ROOM

During our study in the thatched foyer in Barhir Dar, Bob began to bring forth numerous connecting Scriptures to support Isaiah 18 about the location of the throne, as well as what that *present*, or gift, will be. It quickly became evident that we were dealing with something at the time beyond our traditional understanding, but one that demanded more Scripture to confirm his comments.

One of those Scriptures came in the prophecy of Ezekiel:

> *And the glory of the LORD came into the house*
> *by the way of the gate whose prospect is toward*
> *the east. So, the spirit took me up, and brought*
> *me into the inner court; and, behold, the glory*
> *of the LORD filled the house. And I heard him*
> *speaking unto me out of the house; and the man*
> *stood by me. And he said unto me, Son of man,*
> *the place of my throne, and the place of the*
> *soles of my feet, where I will dwell in the midst*
> *of the children of Israel for ever, and my holy*
> *name, shall the house of Israel no more defile,*
> *neither they, nor their kings, by their whoredom,*
> *nor by the carcases of their kings in their high*
> *places.* (Ezekiel 43:4-7)

These verses reveal a prophetic place upon Christ's return to take over the third temple in Jerusalem, and more precisely, the inner court of the Holy of Holies where His throne will be placed. Never in the history of any king did they reign on the throne from inside the temple. Bob, along with many others have stated this, and with my research that is fact. They always took their place of rule from their own thrones within their own palace or castle. This verse specifically is talking about the throne, or the Mercy Seat, being placed inside the temple upon Jesus' return, and His ruling from the Holy of Holies on that throne where He will place the souls of His feet and reign from there forever. We know of the time period, upon His return to claim the throne forever, because Ezekiel describes the time when there will be no more defilement or sin during this reign.

This verse brings to light the days that are to come, when Jesus makes His appearance and what His Throne will appear as. Placing this next to Isaiah 18, it brings us closer to piecing together those events that are yet to come. Could this have been part of what God revealed to Him on Tana Kirkos? We know that God rested on the Mercy Seat, His throne, on the island and taught Jesus from there during the three months and ten days of prayer and teaching. It leads to speculation on the overall knowledge that was given to Jesus at this meeting, and to what extent He was preparing when He left.

Another Scripture that may give us a look into when this return will take place, comes to us in Mark:

> *And then shall they see the Son of man coming in the clouds with great power and glory. And then shall he send his angels, and shall gather together his elect from the four winds, from the uttermost part of the earth to the uttermost part of heaven.* (Mark 13:24-27)

ZEPHANIAH AND THE ROYAL PROCESSION

During our gathering of study in Bahir Dar during that first trip, we were all obviously growing tired from nearly a week of non-stop travel during this expedition. You could tell we were all wearing down, but you also could see the thrill that we all needed more. Regardless of the fatigue, Bob continued to make sure we had uncovered and been educated about in previous times. Regardless of the fatigue, he continued to make sure we had complete knowledge of the Scripture to support this theory on the Ark and its relevance and relationship to Ethiopia.

Now we looked into the Scripture from Zephaniah, which once again brings to the forefront a special offering from the people of Ethiopia:

> *From beyond the rivers of Ethiopia my suppliants, even the daughter of my dispersed, shall bring mine offering…* (Zephaniah 3:10)

This Scripture moved us all. Earlier in the day we had taken the long journey through the desert from Gondar to Barhir Dar. Before leaving Gondar, we had the honor of meeting the lady who is one of the remaining Falashian Jews in Ethiopia. When reading the Scriptures in Zephaniah, one can't help but wonder if a descendent of Mary from Gondar could have a direct hand in bringing forth the Throne back to Jerusalem when it refers to *the daughter of my dispersed*. But what's even more compelling is the way the Ark and Mercy Seat will be returned. If you separate the word *bring* in this text to a translational context, you will start to see a procession opened up, much the same as you would see in Axum during the Timkat ceremony. Could this ceremony possibly even be a yearly rehearsal, if you will, to the events to come somewhere in the future?

Bring in this text is taken from the Hebrew word "*jaw-bal*" which means to "bring forth" or to "lead forth" in a ceremonial type procession with pomp and circumstance. Sitting under a thatched roof in the middle of Ethiopia, along the banks of a lake that claims to have housed the Ark for hundreds of years, it seemed as though things were really "clicking" in my brain at this point. I realized I may have witnessed a yearly practice of the *when it's time* return of the throne of Christ from the people of Ethiopia, to the King of Kings in the house of the Lord in Jerusalem.

Had these people always recognized this ceremony, or were we the ones who have never picked up on this procession. During the Eve of Timkat, which is again claimed to be the celebration of the baptism of Jesus (among other speculations), the monks and priests carry out a replica ark, or Talbot, covered in a jeweled covering. They parade it from the Saint Mary of Zion Church through the streets to a makeshift tabernacle where they place it in the Holy of Holies of the replica tabernacle. They do this dressed in the ceremonial Levite style robes and gowns while blowing trumpets, pounding drums, and clanging sistras. We know from Isaiah 18, *All ye inhabitants of the world, and dwellers on the earth, see ye, when he lifteth up an ensign on the mountains; and when he bloweth a trumpet, hear ye*, which states that when the *present* leaves Ethiopia, that a sign will be shown in the mountains and all the world will hear the trumpets blow. Could this be a secretive rehearsal for this day? Many there claim that it is that practice session that Ethiopia prepares for. Nevertheless, we were enlightened by the Scriptures according to our understanding. They were beginning to unravel the mystery of the sign, the present of the returning throne, and the procession that will celebrate the Mercy Seat's travel to the inner court of the third temple in Jerusalem, *place of my throne, and the place of the soles of my feet.*

The Scripture to back these theories is overwhelming, as we found in various other places including Psalm 68:29, *Because of thy temple at Jerusalem shall kings bring presents unto thee.* Once again, the word "*jaw-bal*" comes into play with the word *bring.* It appears as though the nations will return implements of the tabernacle, but Ethiopia will be bringing the Throne of God. It's somewhat mind blowing, but after returning to the United States I quickly found that this would all precede further evidence to qualify the truth between God the Father and God the Son on the island. It seems as though the entire journey may have been a topic on the island for all of the future events still to come.

REIGNING FROM THE THRONE

More evidence of Scripture foretells the building of the temple and the overall presence of Christ taking up His throne there:

> *And speak unto him, saying, Thus speaketh the LORD of hosts, saying, Behold the man whose name is The BRANCH; and he shall grow up*

> *out of his place, and he shall build the temple of*
> *the LORD: Even he shall build the temple of the*
> *LORD; and he shall bear the glory, and shall*
> *sit and rule upon his throne; and he shall be a*
> *priest upon his throne: and the counsel of peace*
> *shall be between them both.* (Zechariah 6:12, 13)

There is no doubt that when that day arrives there will be no question that Jesus has taken rule and from where He will reign. Scripture is clear several times over staking this claim. My mind returned to Axum once again. One day while in this humble place, we were granted the honor of receiving a blessing from Guardian of the Ark, the man who gives his life inside the enclosure of the Saint Mary of Zion Church to guard it, and another blessing later in the day by Narub, the high priest of Axum. When we quietly met with the Guardian inside the iron fence of the church, we were less than twenty yards from the corner of the building's chamber which they claim contains the Ark of the Covenant.

The possibility that the throne which God sat upon, the Mercy Seat that He met with His Son upon at Tana Kirkos, the place between the two cherubim that face each other, and what could be the future throne of Jesus Himself in Jerusalem, might just have been a few yards from me in this small building. This thought literally brought shivers up my spine. Could I have been wrong all these years? Had tradition clouded me so strongly that I was unable to see what God was showing me so plainly? From this point on, I decided that my mind, my heart, and my trust were going into whatever direction God had in store for me. After that night of Bible study, I was thankful I made that commitment, because it was the next day that we ventured to the island of Tana Kirkos, and my true adventure really began.

ETHIOPIAN EUNICH

This account of the Ethiopian eunuch is another wonderful example of a biblical event presented in great detail, but with the true purpose possibly overlooked. When Luke described the events of Phillip and his ministry in Luke 8, he gave a tremendous amount of time to one particular person in this passage. The Ethiopian Eunuch has been the example for many pastors over the ages as the perfect standard for salvation and the immersed water baptism. What could possibly be overlooked is Luke's apparent clue to the importance of this man and the story's relevance to the Ark of the Covenant's location?

Whenever I come across a biblical event that gives great detail, I become inquisitive why God allowed this much information to be given. I had always pondered this detail, but had fallen into the accepted tradition of what this Scripture was intended to be used for. That tradition, of course, was only to explain salvation and baptism to a possible new believer in Christ.

> *And the angel of the Lord spake unto Philip,*
> *saying, Arise, and go toward the south unto*

the way that goeth down from Jerusalem unto Gaza, which is desert. And he arose and went: and, behold, a man of Ethiopia, an eunuch of great authority under Candace queen of the Ethiopians, who had the charge of all her trea- sure, and had come to Jerusalem for to wor- ship, Was returning, and sitting in his chariot read Esaias the prophet. Then the Spirit said unto Philip, Go near, and join thyself to this chariot. And Philip ran thither to him, and heard him read the prophet Esaias, and said, Understandest thou what thou readest? And he said, How can I, except some man should guide me? And he desired Philip that he would come up and sit with him. The place of the scripture which he read was this, He was led as a sheep to the slaughter; and like a lamb dumb before his shearer, so opened he not his mouth: In his humiliation his judgment was taken away: and who shall declare his generation? for his life is taken from the earth. And the eunuch answered Philip, and said, I pray thee, of whom spea- keth the prophet this? of himself, or of some other man? Then Philip opened his mouth, and began at the same scripture, and preached unto him Jesus. And as they went on their way, they came unto a certain water: and the eunuch said, See, here is water; what doth hinder me to be

> *baptized? And Philip said, If thou believest with all thine heart, thou mayest. And he answered and said, I believe that Jesus Christ is the Son of God. And he commanded the chariot to stand still: and they went down both into the water, both Philip and the eunuch; and he baptized him. And when they were come up out of the water, the Spirit of the Lord caught away Philip, that the eunuch saw him no more: and he went on his way rejoicing.* (Acts 8:26-39)

Yes, it is a beautiful historical account of the acceptance of Christ followed by baptism. But what if there is more to this story as Bob had stated in our study in Bahir Dar? What if this detail was to give us another clue into where the Ark ended up, which in turn gives us more evidence of God's meeting with Jesus on Tana Kirkos Island? As history shows, there were a series of women warriors who held the office of independent rulers known as Kandakes, or Candaces, from around 345 B.C. to 314 A.D. in the area known as Ethiopia. These were spear holding, armored warriors who led the armies, and if killed, would leave the throne to her husband and son *(ref. 22, 23, 24)*.

In the time of Phillip, Queen Candice could possibly have been one of these warrior queens named Amantitere who ruled from 22 to 41 A.D. in Ethiopia *(ref. 25, 26)*. Regardless, this queen had appointed the Ethiopian Eunuch to be in charge of her treasury, which gave him great authority in her kingdom. As Phillip arrived on the desert road known as Gaza, we see this Ethiopian sitting in his chariot, confused about what he was reading in a large scroll from Isaiah describing the characteristics of Christ in chapter 53. Was the confusion of the Eunuch based on his visit to Jerusalem, only to find it somewhat depressed? He probably had arrived in Jerusalem expecting to see some kind of celebration for the risen Savior. This may have led to his confusion when Phillip saw him pondering the words Isaiah.

Without a doubt, this Ethiopian, along with his queen, would have read Isaiah 52 giving a look into the events leading up to, and possibly following Isaiah 53. But then a quick look at a verse in Isaiah 52, may give us a little more insight into the purpose of this Eunuch:

> *Depart ye, depart ye, go ye out from thence,*
> *touch no unclean thing; go ye out of the midst*
> *of her; be ye clean, that bear the vessels of the*
> *LORD.* (Isaiah 52:11)

Could this be what the Eunuch took as a sign that he was to go to Jerusalem to see if the holy artifact that Queen Candace held in her treasury, needed to be returned to the Christ at Zion? Scripture tells us that they are to depart and touch no unclean thing, which perfectly describes why Candice would have sent the Eunuch, simply because of his purity. And since this Eunuch was the keeper of the treasures of the queen, could the reference to *the one who bears the vessels of the LORD* be a direct tie to the Ethiopian's claim that they were holding, and possibly still are, the Ark of the Covenant, and the Mercy Seat?

Let's also take a moment to look closer at the Ethiopian mentioned. Knowing that he was the keeper of the treasury, we can assume that he was no "normal" eunuch. During my study in the library at the Hebrew Union College in Cincinnati one particular day, I was addressed by an astute older gentleman that saw my close study. I had a stack of books on the table and he inquired about my research. As I had the books opened, searching for anything I could find about Old Testament uses of a eunuch in the ancient world, the man asked if my study had anything to do with the Ethiopian in Acts Chapter 8. I told him that it did, but I wanted to see what the uses were for eunuchs leading up to the time of the New Testament. He, being a Messianic Jew himself, was quick to point out to me that I may be looking at this in the wrong text. He showed me in another book (of the many he had with him) that the eunuch may be a more important member of the queen's inner realm than than what we interpret in the Bible. He said, "You must look at this. He was keeping her treasury. Do you think he was just some eunuch watching over the most important holdings of the country?" I shook my head from side-to-side. He went on, "This man was a man of importance and in the old Hebrew he would have be more known closer to that of a general who would have been castrated for the queen's protection. That would lead us to believe that when this was translated that the Ethiopian man lost a little clout by just being called a eunuch." This made a great deal of sense and that explanation would be more believable to the reason why this man would have been of such an importance to the Ethiopian queen.

Upon a return journey the next year in Ethiopia, I spoke with Sisay, the young man who I built a great, trusted relationship with, to look into this deeper. He came back with the same information, that in the Ethiopian Amharic translation he was known as the "jandereba," or to say, the general. This all makes more sense to the understanding that the queen would never send just anyone to investigate such an important event, but to send the general, who was the keeper or watchman of her treasury and the Ark of the Covenant.

As we know, as noted in the Scripture, the Ethiopian accepts the salvation through Christ, and Phillip takes him down into the water to be baptized. Once realizing that the Mercy Seat was not needed at this time, and with his new-found assurance, he returned to Ethiopia rejoicing and telling others of his conversion. This again raises a question why the detail of this story, both in Acts 8 and Isaiah, if there is not more meaning to it. If it were only needed for a salvation and baptism experience, much of this Scripture would not have been needed. Maybe the Lord had more to share than we are given to believe. Maybe this gives us a closer glimpse into the importance of this ancient land of Ethiopia once again. It also opens up the doors to see the importance of Queen Candice, and her role in previous events of the Bible, but that's for another day.

HIDDEN WHERE NO ONE COULD CARE TO LOOK

Looking back on this ancient land of the northern highlands of Ethiopia, we can see why this would be the perfect hiding place to one of the Bible's greatest treasures. The difference from this treasure and any other is that the Ark of the Covenant played such a great role in the Old Testament, and then is simply gone and mysteriously not mentioned again. That is, until the time that it will be needed again. So why would Ethiopia be the perfect place to hide this mysterious artifact? The answer is simple: So no one would desire to pursue it in a land that the world looks upon as a place of poverty, disease, and starvation. And to the world's standards, they wouldn't believe it was there either.

Yes, Ethiopia has continually experienced famine that seems to hasten the demise of these people through not only starvation, but also disease. Over seventy percent of this nation is starving and below the poverty line. Many perish from malaria, and due to the lack of resources, people are unable to acquire the medication to treat or prevent this disease that is spread through the abundance of mosquitoes. Only seventeen percent of the nation has access to clean drinking water which is directly due to the lack of rain in this arid region. With that statistic added to the widespread cases of HIV, tuberculosis, and other diseases, it doesn't take long to realize this is not your ideal site for persuing ancient biblical hidden resources or for taking a family vacation. That is until you get to know and see the resilience of the people there.

One of the most interesting statements that I heard came from a young man I spoke with in Axum, when I asked why there is suffering in many ways there. "Mr. Jim, you must think about it this way; you have your cars, homes, and many things which we do not have. We only have God, and then we have our family. That's really all we need." The Ethiopians in this region have accepted that this is the way it has to be in order to be the keepers, or custodians, of the Ark and Mercy Seat. They believe that they have been given this task and must suffer in order to be somewhat left alone until the appointed time has come. To the people of Axum, although there is tourism created there from gawkers at the church of the Ark and sites in the area, they have been given the duty to guard what they claim God has entrusted to them. And the Ark and Mercy Seat may not be the only secrets they are guarding.

ONE LAST THOUGHT: WHY ETHIOPIA WHEN EGYPT IS ONLY MENTIONED?

In the Bible Scriptures, we learn in Matthew 2:13 that the holy family is only mentioned to have gone into Egypt:

> *"And when they were departed, behold, the angel*
> *of the Lord appeareth to Joseph in a dream,*
> *saying, Arise, and take the young child and his*
> *mother, and flee into Egypt,"*

This again is a fulfillment of the prophecy of Hosea 11:1, *"and called my son out of Egypt."* This is a confirmed cross-reference to this being written in Matthew 2:15. But, again, remember that the Apostle John tells us in 21:25 that there are many other things that Jesus did that are not mentioned in the Scriptures.

During one of my research projects in Egypt, my historian friend, Samer from Cairo, brought up an interesting truth to this idea, that as I began to look further into it, the theory became more of a possibility. The reason why Egypt is only mentioned is backed by a strong idea of why we don't see Ethiopia located in modern-day Bibles in the maps sections, and why the name Cush is replacing the name of Ethiopia. The darker skinned people of Africa have been nearly eliminated from most writings, maps, and importance. Again, look in your modern maps of the Bible; Ethiopia is gone. Look at descriptions of Ethiopia in the Bible; replaced by the name Cush or other descriptions, which adds to the confusion. Look at the theological discriptions of Ethiopian; they completely have replaced it with other lands.

This theory goes back to the European translators of the Bible as we notice people like the Ethiopian eunuch in Acts chapter 8 (vs. 27-39). Here we learn that a very important man of Ethiopia is sitting in a chariot reading a manuscript of Isaiah. This man is working for the queen of Ethiopia. First; a simple Ethiopian eunuch is not going to be sitting in a chariot in Gaza reading a scroll of the book of Isaiah, after just visiting Jerusalem. He's the keeper of the queen's treasures according to the Bible, so this is not just some ordinary man. But yet, we see his name and importance downgraded to a simple eunuch. In translation, most likely this man was a general or high priest for the queen.

Let's look at the queen mentnioned in Acts chapter 8 (vs. 27). In the Bible her name is mentioned as Candace. After spending many years working in Ethiopia, I have found many things, and visited with thousands upon thousands of people, and nowhere have I ever found any women named Candice anywhere. What I did find is the name Candace was a European translation for a queen name Mendeke. And this is only a couple of examples of the many oversights when it comes to the Biblical Africa, all the way back to Garden of Eden in Genesis.

With that said, this same idea might be in play here as well when it comes to only Egypt being mentioned in the holy family's flight into this African land. During my time in Egypt, it's quick to see that they consider themselves as a Middle-Eastern area land, not African, even though they are just as much a part of it as Ethiopia. Understanding this may give us a strong insight into the only mention of Egypt.

After Moses' conquest of Ethiopia, this idea stood well in place that Ethiopia was somewhat under the rule of Egypt. Over time this theory begins to collapse with the growing powers of Ethiopia rising, but their land masses were dwindling. Thus, the Nubians (southern Egypt), and areas which later became Sudan began to fall away from the Ethiopian kingdom. Thus, the theory that early Bible translators may have considered Ethiopia under Egyptian rule may play a part in the lack of mentioning them in the trek for the holy family through Egypt into Ethiopia for the Messiah's fulfillment with God the Father.

This is a great theory, but we have no physical information to base this on other than the obvious removals or downgrading of mainland Africa from the Bible translations. Then, of course, the other theory, with a great deal of fact is again John's mention in chapter 21:25 of his Gospel that there are many things that Jesus did that are not mentioned within the pages of the Bible. This could very well be one of those things He did, to protect the place, the people, and proof left behind until the time God needed it to be revealed to the world.

Chapter 13:

LINKING THE PUZZLE TOGETHER

THEORIES RUN WILD IN a situation like this. Without actually being there, we may never know what actually took place during Jesus' time on the mysterious island of Tana Kirkos. But, without a doubt, we can assume some things by reviewing the facts of this miraculous journey. Just as Jesus said when the Pharisees asked Him to denounce His followers from crying out His Holiness in Luke 19:40, *I tell you that, if these should hold their peace, the stones would immediately cry out,* I can't help but feel that the incredible faith of the "guardians of the secrets" of the land of Ethiopia will once again cry out the holiness of Christ under the trust that God has bestowed on this land. Yes, they have their downfalls, but they also continue to lay claim to some of the most incredible artifacts and untold secrets that the world has ever known. I also believe that Ethiopia holds many more secrets that haven't even emerged yet.

As we examine the pieces of this jigsaw puzzle, we discover many interesting, amazing, and just plain and simple stunning facts crying out from the stones in the ancient land of Ethiopia. In order to comprehend the complete implications of this story, let's take some time to put these facts together so we can sense the magnitude of the evidence.

THE ANGEL'S WARNING TO FLEE:

Once again, the story begins with the appearance of the angel to Joseph in Matthew 2:13 to warn him of the impending "slaughter of the innocence" with King Herod's fear, search, and massacre of all the male children from the ages two and under. With fear and determination, Joseph follows the request of the angel, packs up his family, and journeys to the preset trail for them into Egypt.

DISCOVERING EGYPT:

The incredible detailed history of the flight of the holy family into Egypt can be found in a series of recorded documents along the trail of this ancient land, as well as in the Coptic oral records passed down through the ages, along with Muslim hidden manuscripts as recorded by the Egyptians, and by what was taught by Mark (the gospel writer) whose ministry was primarily in Egypt, including a possible seminary, or school, for teaching and discipling in Alexandria. The trail is specific and carries a great deal of merit, considering that many of the churches, ancient paintings, and historic accounts date back centuries. Many traditionalists struggle with anything that doesn't have a firm foundation in the Scripture. I guess that's what changed my thinking along this trail. Sometimes God will work through those who may believe but don't fully understand. That's exactly what He did with me. I was a traditionalist who, through a window of doubt, had a glimmer of hope that God would share a secret with the rest of the world through that hope. I still follow many of the old beliefs, but have realized that when God has something to reveal, He will change the minds of those He has chosen to complete the tasks. This all came true for me when I began to study the trail of the holy family in Egypt, and then journey through the hidden lands of Ethiopia. I learned that we can't take what man always says as the gospel, but when God is involved, we have to keep our minds open to the heavenly possibility.

VENTURING SOUTH:

In one of the most telling twists in this story, we see the holy family, after a montage of stops in northern Egypt, make a turn to the south by meeting up with the Nile River, and charting a due course into what is known as Upper Egypt, which is actually to the south. Even when questioned, historians, priests, and monks in Egypt really have no explanation for this turn other than the pending threat of Herod's soldiers finding their location. Understandably, in the northern regions of Egypt that makes some sense. But when you look at the facts that Herod didn't even know who he was looking for, thus the slaughter of possibly thousands of innocent children (Matthew 2:16), there's a great deal of suspicion why the holy family necessarily headed due south, and continued on the journey. This should raise an eyebrow, and give you an "Ah ha" moment to this question.

FOLLOWING THE GREAT NILE RIVER:

Another interesting fact is that if Herod's soldiers would have been hot on the holy family's trail, wouldn't it make more sense to move away from the populated areas of the Nile River and disappear into a remote village in the desert or an oasis region in Egypt? But, as we have learned, that's not what happened. They traveled from town to town with Jesus making known His entry as idols fell, and some of the gods-worshipping priests became fearful at His appearance. In other words, there was no hiding that Jesus was who He claimed to be. Even their arrival in Muharraq should raise red flags because of its far southern location in Egypt. Why would God allow them to travel, strain, and venture so far away from home in order to be called back when they arrived there? Could there have been further instructions? And why was it the Nile they stayed so closely to? The answers seem overwhelming, but very likely that the holy family may have stopped in Muharraq, liked it, and then returned to it after venturing down into Ethiopia for the prophetic meeting.

ETHIOPIA'S TREASURES:

The treasures that deal with the Ark of the Covenant, the Mercy Seat, and the so-called missing pieces, seem to fit together perfectly. And what is most interesting is that it appears as though the Ethiopians themselves haven't even put the pieces all together, nor do they feel they need to. They seem to take their divinely appointed commission for granted, in some ways. We find that they are guarding a lot more than the Ark, a missing link to some of the mysteries of Christ not shared in the Scriptures. Maybe these are the untold stories that John refers to in 21:25. Let's look at some of these treasures together.

TRUMPETS:

In Axum, Ethiopia they claim to have the ancient pounded silver trumpets of Moses mentioned in Numbers chapter 10. These trumpets were used to calling the people to the tabernacle following God's appearance on the Throne on the Day of Atonement. These trumpets were blown to announce the entry of the Ark to a new location, and will one day sound again to announce its return to the third temple (Isaiah 18:7). Today, the Ethiopians claim to have these trumpets housed in the treasury in Axum. The second temple was prophesized to be destroyed, and it was in August of 70 A.D. by the Roman general named Titus. The trumpets that we actually saw match perfectly the trumpets described in the Bible. When the second temple was built, the ceremonial items that had been taken were replicated and placed in their respective positions in the new temple. We can compare these trumpets to the replicas that Titus marched through the streets of Rome after his destruction of the second temple, as carved in the Arch of Titus that still stands in the

Italian city today. We see a perfect match to those etched in Rome to the trumpets in Axum within the treasury. This event was horrific and vividly depicted by Jewish historian Flavius Josephus, who was in Jerusalem at the time of the capture of the city and when the demise of the second temple took place in flames: *The Romans, though it was a terrible struggle to collect the timber, raised their platforms in twenty-one days, having as described before stripped the whole area in a circle round the town to a distance of ten miles. The countryside like the City was a pitiful sight; for where once there had been a lovely vista of woods and parks there was nothing but desert and stumps of trees. No one—not even a foreigner—who had seen the Old Judea and the glorious suburbs of the City, and now set eyes on her present desolation, could have helped sighing and groaning at so terrible a change; for every trace of beauty had been blotted out by war, and nobody who had known it in the past and came upon it suddenly would have recognized the place: when he was already there he would still have been looking for the City (Ref. 27).* Inside the temple were replicas of the original "treasures" which were taken and paraded by Titus in celebration of his victory. But still today, the original trumpets appear to be secured away in Axum, Ethiopia.

ARK OF THE COVENANT:

Without a doubt, the Ark of the Covenant is the most treasured, and sought-after artifact in history. The Ark of the Covenant, with the Mercy Seat, was built to house the Holy Law of God, the Ten Commandments, during the time of Moses. It rested in a series of makeshift tabernacles until it came to its home in the first temple of Solomon. After that, the mystery of its whereabouts is shrouded in assumptions, theories, and turmoil. Biblical accounts disregard many of those theories, but the clues leading the Ark and the Mercy Seat to Ethiopia seem to be indisputable. We would have to concur that the Ethiopians claim to be the guardians of this holy object. This claim appears to be authentic, but only time will tell if their claim is divinely appointed.

THE GUARDIAN:

Top and bottom photos show Jim with Sisay and the
Guardian of the Ark of the Covenant in Axum, Ethiopia.

In Axum and in Saint Mary of Zion Church, the Guardian of
the Ark lives his life to worship, and to guard this holy object
they claim to have. Do they have it? I can't answer that, and
no one else can either, except for the Guardian himself. He was
chosen for his purity as a child, trained, and then takes his position as the Guardian and keeper of the Ark. He will guard it with
his life until he chooses another Guardian before his passing.

This man, considered to be extremely holy in nature, surrenders his life to stay within the area of the high iron fence that surrounds this small church in order to pray and protect their claim. He seems to have a loneliness about him, but a peacefulness that surrounds as he wanders the perimeter of the grounds. This should raise an obvious question, why someone would give his life to guard something that wasn't there? Maybe this should make us think strongly about what they claim to possess.

THEIR FAITH:

The people of Ethiopia, pledging that they have the Holy Ark and that God has entrusted them throughout the ages with secrets, have an enduring and constant faith. As I stood on a cliff and oversaw the people day after day coming out of the mountains to worship, sometimes for hours, I couldn't help but feel embarrassed about the limited time we give to God daily. In many cases, their worship begins in the early morning hours, when the wooden and animal hide bass drums begin to pound and the chanting worship and prayers begin to amplify over the land. When you see people plant their faces in the sand praying for hours on end, you begin to feel the desire for God's own heart that these people routinely seek. Still today, the Ethiopians carry an Old Testament faith that is an example to the world of their dedication to Him.

THE FORBIDDEN ISLAND OF TANA KIRKOS:

This mysterious island is one of the most amazing places I have ever witnessed during my world travels. Hidden some three and a half hours from the city of Barhir Dar in the massive expanse of Lake Tana, this Ethiopian treasure appears to have been the site to a holy meeting with profound significance. The island was not only the resting place for the Ark of the Covenant for nearly 800 years until King Ezana came to claim it for the kingdom of Axum, but from all indications, it was also the exact place that Father God chose to reveal wisdom and grace to a young Jesus during their meeting on this holy piece of rock. The intense secrecy on this island never really hit home until I met the Ethiopians in the Library in Cincinnati. Their shock that I had been on Tana Kirkos to photograph these pages brought a new perspective to the term *forbidden*. It was as though this place was intentionally shielded from the rest of the world, and in its own right, it really was. The world was not welcomed here, and I thank the Lord for leading me to this incredible place to renew a faith in me that was now beyond anything I had ever experienced before.

GUARDIAN MONKS & PRIESTS:

Just as in Old Testament times, the treasures of the Lord have been guarded both from mankind and from time. The ironic part of this mystery, now with the exposure of the ancient gravesite, is that we now know they have been repeating this process for centuries before. The holy men who guard this island have been carefully chosen at a very early age to carry out the centuries-old duties as guardians of the secrets of this island. Only a select few are permitted to visit this island, and even fewer may pass through the jungle to the area considered to be "holy ground." Once chosen, these monks will give their lives to raise their crops, worship, and protect its age-old secrets. Their abiding faith and their dedication to serving the Lord is noteworthy. They live in small huts, not much bigger than a closet, they suffer through ailments and injuries without medication, they spend each day of their lives tending to crops, and they worship long hours in the temple. Their endurance is phenomenal, and their heart for the Lord is unmistakable. They take their God-given assignment as guardians very seriously, but they will show their hospitality to share a cup of coffee or a piece of injera bread as a symbol of friendship and peace. These men are warriors of their faith who have taught me a great deal about to my own worship to the Lord.

EAGLES:

The first thing I noticed when I came to the island of Tana Kirkos were the two white and black eagles that perched seemingly to guard the island from way above. Aba Gabriel said to me that ever since he has been on this island, which has been for a very long time, these majestic and beautiful birds have always stood watch in the trees. Ironically, the eagles stand guard above the site where most of the ancient Holy events took place. It's relative to the Scripture in Isaiah 40:31 that states, *But they that wait upon the LORD shall renew their strength; they shall mount up with wings as eagles; they shall run, and not be weary; and they shall walk, and not faint.* In other words, the secrets that this island has guarded for centuries will be revealed, but we must wait for God's timing. When the appointed time arrives, God will put those secrets on the wings of eagles and give them to the world. It's somewhat symbolic, but a vivid reminder that God gives us our portion in His perfect time.

TOMB OF THE PRIEST:

Also on Tana Kirkos is the tomb of the high priest who brought the Ark of the Covenant to this island. Just a few yards past the flat stone surface that held the altar of the Ark of the Covenant are two large boulders forming a "V" shape, filled in with smaller stones to make up the final resting place of the high priest. This rocky grave is a reminder of the accuracy of every detail that Ethiopia guards as evidence to their claims. Today, one can barely see into this grave containing the nearly extinct remains of this priest, along with pottery shards that accompanied him during the burial. Again, interesting to note, the place where the Ark was lifted from the waters some fifty feet below, is just a few steps past the grave site. This adds further validity to the ever-growing evidence on Tana Kirkos. Just think, the remains could well be the high priest who carried out the Holy atonement ceremony in the presence of God!

THE ROCK ALTAR OF THE ARK AND THRONE:

On the cliff where the Ark is claimed to have rested for hundreds of years is a flat stone surface measuring to the perfect measurements of the Ark of the Covenant. After pulling up old grass off the slab, pushing dirt, and throwing off the old leaves, I had discovered seven carved out indentions in the stone, measuring the accurate distance of the resting feet of the Ark of the Covenant. And the ever-mounting pile of evidence in this research was growing. In this same place, Jesus allegedly knelt, prayed, and listened to His Father as He was filled with the wisdom for His future ministry. If this claim is truth, and it could very well be, then this particular spot on this island conceals undeniable historical importance and scriptural reverence. This site could well be the exact location where God the Father and God the Son met.

TABERNACLE SOCKETS:

Just a few feet away from the slab where the Ark rested, you will find the first of the large carved out sockets in the rock that held the poles of the Tabernacle as described in the book shown to us by the Aba and in God's Word. These pole sockets would have held the tabernacle in place, and they stretch up the cliff side. Bob Cornuke discovered these pole sockets several years earlier, which add to the accuracy of the claims and secrets of this island. With the breezes blowing across the lake and up to the top of this island, there had to be some way of anchoring the tabernacle that is claimed to have rested here in place. This is another confirmation of the claim of the accurate truth. Although two of the sockets plummeted to the waters below and were cut off and returned later, the vision of a once holy tabernacle resting here is well within the possibility of truth, seeing the evidence that has accumulated over time.

SACRIFICIAL STONE BOWL:

After the footholds of the Ark, this is one piece that the Aba is very quick to show to newcomers in our group when we arrive. Just a few yards from the resting spot of the Ark is a small metal building; inside is a large stone basin with a carved-out bowl within the rock, which they claim is the bowl that the blood was poured into for the sacrifice. Again, the Ark was located on the cliff just yards away. It's interesting to see this artifact, because it would serve no other purpose other than for something ceremonial. Now, with all of the evidence in place, this would indicate that this spot is where the high priest would have dipped the blood sacrifice for the atonement ceremony upon the Ark of the Covenant.

SOLOMON'S TEMPLE TREASURES:

Also on the island of Tana Kirkos are the implements used in the sacrificial ceremonies of the Day of Atonement. Are these the same implements used in the ceremonial efforts in Solomon's Temple? Only time will tell, although testing has taken place on the island indicating that the implements were correct in dating to the period, but the larger copper/bronze bowl may be from around the time of Christ. When you consider the timing of the Ark on the island, then this would continue to show the accuracy of the claims, since it wasn't taken from this spot until three hundred years after Jesus was on the cross. These are not treasures of wealth, but the treasures of the tabernacle which had no other purpose than for these ceremonies. We were privileged to behold those artifacts while in this small treasury room. Every one of these items confirms that the Ark could very well have been entrusted to these people, and even more specifically the sacred meeting on the island.

BREASTPLACE HARNESS OF THE HIGH PRIEST:

Jim holds the ephod harness of the high priest used during the ancient
Day of Atonement ceremony at the Ark.

And thou shalt take the garments, and put upon
Aaron the coat, and the robe of the ephod, and
the ephod, and the breastplate, and gird him with
the curious girdle of the ephod...(Exodus 29:5.)

250

One of the most shocking items in the treasury was what they claimed to be the remains of the ephod harness that the high priest would have worn during his entry into the holy of holies for the atonement service. The cage-like, presumably bronze harness made of flattened metal, fit over the shoulders and would have been the undergarment frame to the cloth with the twelve stones of the twelve tribes of Israel attached to it. If this is truly what they claim, then it is an astonishing find, knowing it would have been worn in the presence of God's appearance on the Throne. Holding this artifact in my hands literally gave me chills, and one of the men on our exploration team said that my face turned white when Aba handed it to me. In reality, much of what was handed to me in this small room was overwhelming. Just the overall thought of what was in my hands and what we were in the presence of, was taking my emotions to an unprecedented level. All I know is that this harness of the breastplate has been in the presence of God Himself.

SACRIFICIAL CLEANSING BOWL AND STAND:

Again, a presumably copper/bronze, heavily tarnished, artifact that fits the description in the Bible of the bowl for the cleansing of the high priest before entering the Holy of Holies.

And the LORD spake unto Moses, saying, Thou
shalt also make a laver of brass, and his foot
also of brass, to wash withal: and thou shalt put
it between the tabernacle of the congregation

and the altar, and thou shalt put water therein...
(Exodus 30:17-18)

And Moses took the anointing oil, and anointed the tabernacle and all that was therein, and sanctified them. And he sprinkled thereof upon the altar seven times, and anointed the altar and all his vessels, both the laver and his foot, to sanctify them... (Leviticus 8:10-11)

This bowl rests upon a perfectly fitted metal stand that has collapsed over time due to the age and weight of the bowl. This was another artifact that has no other purpose except the one they claim.

AARON'S ALMOND BUD MEAT FORKS:

And it came to pass, that on the morrow Moses went into the tabernacle of witness; and, behold, the rod of Aaron for the house of Levi was budded, and brought forth buds, and bloomed blossoms, and yielded almonds... (Numbers 17:8)

One of the most recognizable pieces that links these items in the island's treasures to the Day of Atonement ceremony is the almond topped meat forks for the burnt offering ceremonies. These long two-pronged meat forks contain the design of an almond flower at the top. This is a direct witness to the theme of the almond bud that God blessed Aaron's staff with; it later became a signature of Aaron's position. This is one of those pieces that you question all the details: a four-foot metal fork on a remote island with an almond flower bud engraved into the top of the joint between the prongs. The appearance of the almond was a deciding factor confirming the authenticity of all the other artifacts shown to us on the island, and directly dates these objects to the time of the ceremonies of sacrifice.

BURNT OFFERING HOOKS:

> *And the priest shall put some of the blood upon the horns of the altar of sweet incense before the LORD, which is in the tabernacle of the congregation: and shall pour all the blood of the bullock at the bottom of the altar of the burnt offering, which is at the door of the tabernacle of the congregation.* (Leviticus 4:7)

The meat hooks for the sacrificial blood and the burnt offerings are again made of sturdy metal, and have a collection of hooks on them in order to hang the meat that was prepared for the burnt offerings to the Lord. This would have also been where the blood would have been collected below for the sacrificial bowl. These are perfect examples of the detail that the guardians of the island wouldn't need to confirm, but because of their overt innocence, add to the pieces of the puzzle. Many of the items aren't really needed to justify their claim but do lend themselves to the overall authenticity of the artifacts.

PLACE OF A MOTHER'S PRAYERS:

High on the top of the cliff overlooking the treasury, a distance away from the resting place of the Ark of the Covenant where her Son would have been with the Father, is the prayer rock of Jesus' mother, Mary. The interesting thought to this particular site is that you can see nearly the entire island as well as islands far away from this post. This is also the location of the roosting black and white eagles standing watch over the *holy ground*. The view from this point is spectacular, but the thought that Mary would have knelt here day after day as she prayed for Jesus, is truly inspirational. If only the stone would talk to us now and reveal the events that took place here some two thousand years ago!

WHERE JESUS KNELT:

When I first collapsed on the rock and then discovered the footholds of the Ark of the Covenant, Aba Gabriel said to Misgana (both on their knees at this point now) that I was kneeling on the place where Jesus knelt. When the Aba said this to Misgana, and he translated for me, I was both in confusion and doubt. It is not only spoken of, but documented with evidence from the Aba, and based on the historical account in the ancient book. I will never forget the numbness that overtook my arms and fingers as I fell to my knees, not knowing what had taken place on this exact spot, this stone slab that the Ark of the Covenant had rested on. It was also the exact spot where the young Jesus had taken His position, just like a school boy taking his place at his desk, to learn from God's teaching and absorb the tremendous wisdom we read about in Luke 2:40. I couldn't help but ponder Jesus' reaction to His Father when it was revealed that He would one day be the sacrifice for all mankind. It reminds me of the plea of Christ in the Garden of Gethsemane prior to the arrival of the Roman soldiers with Judas in Matthew:

> *And he went a little further, and fell on his face, and prayed, saying, O my Father, if it be possible, let this cup pass from me: nevertheless not as I will, but as thou wilt.* (Matthew 26:39)

One of the most inspiring moments in my life took place on this rock where some two thousand years earlier Jesus Christ spent three months and ten days in the presence of the Father, in this exact location and on this same spot.

THE PROOF IS IN THE PAGES:

None of this would have been possible if it weren't for the kindness of the Aba and the timely approval of God to reveal the contents of the historical ancient book in the treasury. Resting among the dusty old books, Bibles, and scrolls lay an ancient animal skin writing containing a long-guarded secret of the land of Ethiopia. It was just as the Aba in Cincinnati referred to the contents as "a secret in Ethiopia for thousands of years and few people know about this, about Jesus and Maria coming to this place." By this time, I was well aware that we had been given a great honor to be shown such a document. A piece of ancient history that was to be hidden away until someone was to either stumble across it, or it was to be shown to someone to tell the story. Somehow, that someone just happened to me. Like every person chosen by God for certain purpose, I too, question "why me?" The journey, the events, the people are all pieces of a heavenly puzzle I find myself putting together.

JOHN'S TELLING IN HIS GOSPEL:

During the translation of the ancient writings, one of the more shocking pieces of the text came when I learned that Jesus' disciple, John, was the author of the story. There were two copies of this writing: one was destroyed in the Alexandrian library fire, and the other brought here for safekeeping. The most telling revelation came when the Ethiopian priest in Cincinnati clarified the eight and a half lines that warn about removing, changing, or adding to the pages of the book. When I told the Ethiopian translators that these same warnings were in our Bible, they were quick to tell me that this was written before John wrote the ending to Revelation. Finally, the Aba added that the writings were written down by Prochorus, the deacon chosen in Acts 6, Peter's apprentice, and John's student.

Prochorus is also the main ingredient to the connection of the warning both in this book and in Revelation since he was the one who most likely assisted John on the island of Patmos when the final book of the Bible was recorded.

> *For I testify unto every man that heareth the words of the prophecy of this book, If any man shall add unto these things, God shall add unto him the plagues that are written in this book: And if any man shall take away from the words of the book of this prophecy, God shall take away his part out of the book of life, and out of the holy city, and from the things which are written in this book. He which testifieth these things saith, Surely I come quickly. Amen. Even so, come, Lord Jesus.* (Revelation 22:18-20)

Knowing that this story was given to John by his own mother, Salome, and Mary sometime after Jesus' crucifixion, resurrection, and ascension, added even more credibility to the overwhelming evidence mounting in this story.

THE PLATFORM CRACKS:

> *...and the earth did quake, and the rocks rent;*
> (Matthew 27:51b)

Maybe it's just me, but when you see all of this evidence come together, well, let's just say, it's amazing when God begins to paint the picture right in front of you. This is one of those discoveries that just fit, and when it came to reality it was just a piece of beauty. Sherri had the idea after our first visit ended with my findings of the footholds of the Ark of the Covenant on Tana Kirkos Island. For a number of years, she had been urging me to ask and seek information about what, if anything had happened on the island when Jesus went to the cross and the temple veil ripped. At this same time the Ark of the Covenant, and the Throne of God (the Mercy Seat) was still located on the island. Her feeling was that when Christ went to the cross and gave His last breath, and the Earth shook that something would have happened on the island where God's Throne also rested.

Upon my visit to the island in 2016, I finally remembered what she had asked me to bring up to Aba Gabriel. Without any hesitation, and with a feeling of fulfillment, Aba began to show me the results of that day. First, the two pole holes for that Holy of Holies broke and fell off the side of the mountain, making the tent fall over the Ark and the Throne. Also during the earthquake, the platform that the Ark sat upon cracked, causing the three center footholds to shift slightly to the north. There was no hesitation after I asked the question, the Aba immediately answered and began to demonstrate. This was to show that the Ark and the tabernacle had served its primary purpose, but it was also the beginning of the Ethiopian destiny to protect the Throne of God and keep safe until they will be called upon to return it Christ at His return.

It was a relief to Aba to finally be asked, to Sherri because of the feeling the Lord had given her years earlier, and to me to know that the puzzle was coming together even more than I could have ever imagined. It was also a blessing to have so many others with me when it was revealed to be witness to such an incredible revelation.

CLEARING THE PATH:

The evidence continued to mount, as each step along the path was cleared leading us on an unprecedented adventure. The entire expedition was ordained to make sure that it was presented to the world properly. I see God's hand in each and every piece of this complicated-but revealing-puzzle. This journey started with a family outing in Gatlinburg, Tennessee, to an unusual phone meeting to order a DVD, to an eventual return call back, and then finally to an invitation to be a part of an exploration that would take us by faith to an ancient world. That was followed by fundraisers, meetings with people in need, revelations on the cliffs of Axum, and then eventually arriving in Barhir Dar and traveling by boat to Tana Kirkos Island. But the clearing didn't stop there. Each step was a "dusting off" of the walkway that we were being led to take. There wasn't a hedge along the path except when I would take my eyes from it.

CONFIRMING THE TRANSLATION:

Another part of the "clearing" was the way the translation of the documents came together. After returning, one of our biggest prayers was to be able to find someone to help us translate the ancient language so we could grasp the meaning of the writings. Surely as a result of divine intervention, an aged and knowledgeable Ethiopian priest met with us and obligingly transcribed the words of the pages and removed the blinders from our eyes, thus confirming the claims of the Aba on Tana Kirkos Island. This marked the beginning of an enduring friendship that seems to complete my round-the-world journey.

REVELATION TO THE WORLD:

With verification of all our discoveries and revelations, it was quite evident to me that we needed to share this story with the world. Even though this has been a well-guarded secret to the whereabouts of Christ as a boy, it is also testimony to the fact that when God wants something revealed, He will clear all obstacles to make it happen. The same is true with the footholds of the Ark of the Covenant. It wasn't until I physically collapsed on the spot where Jesus knelt and the Ark rested, that I began clearing the platform of the footholds. It was right before us, but wasn't revealed until God set the plan in motion. This information clarifies multiple questions about the travels of the holy family. What makes this a more incredible discovery is that many so-called historical texts have been written and dismissed because of man's denial that any truth beyond the Bible would be unfounded. Just as historian Jerome, and the translators of the Bible, such as Wycliffe, Martin Luther, and Tyndale only included the divine texts that were consistent with the overall Word of God, the same should be discerned with many of the discovered hidden ancient historical manuscripts to their confirmation, but not as replacement. These men, and many others, were using many of these historical books, but over time, farther away from the original works, man has decided to remove them from any world view.

This takes us back to John 21:25, telling us that there was much more that Jesus did that wasn't recorded in the Scriptures. This may also mean that there was much more written somewhere about those many other things. It did not say that they weren't written down at all. It's the same with the Disciples of Christ and their historical demise. We have historical record of the fate, many times a tragic one, of the Disciples of Christ. Their deaths were recorded, and the historians accept their story in ancient documents, but they weren't included in the Holy Scriptures. Therefore, why can't we accept that there was more to Jesus' life recorded than what the Bible tells us? Or, for that matter, the additional recording of events in the Bible? The Scripture gives us what we need for our lives and salvation, but historical documents give us just that, the history. On the top of a mysterious island, in the middle of a massive lake in Ethiopia, a place mentioned many times in the Scripture, lay an unmistakable secret in history that needed to be revealed, and now it has been.

THE SCRIPTURE LEADS US:

And finally, within the Scripture, we see a young boy who was born to the world in order to save it from the sin that has overcome it, and then He disappears from the pages until we find that He has been filled with wisdom, knowledge, and the grace of God. Then again, Jesus is gone from the Scriptures. Now just maybe with this miraculous find, we have a better idea what happened following His trek into Egypt and beyond and how He obtained the knowledge He would need for all future events that include you and me.

THE LAST PIECE OF THE PUZZLE IN PLACE:

In many ways, we need to open our eyes to what God is revealing all around the world. In the Middle East, there have been more locations and artifacts found in the last several years than any other time in history. So quickly and plentiful, in many cases, we don't hear about them all because the news would be filled with stories of new finds all the time. Besides, that's what the enemy wants, to veer you away from newfound historical biblical truth in order to keep you ignorant of God's fulfilling prophecy. What better way to cause question to those who don't believe in Christ in the first place! If Christians don't believe, then why should anyone else? Maybe that's what we need to really consider in this world of confusion today.

Chapter 14:

LOST YEARS OR NOT?

WERE THE YEARS OF Jesus as a boy really lost? Did He really do anything of significance during those unmentioned years of the Bible? Were His only important and God-like episodes written in the Holy Scriptures we read about today? I believe, along with many others, that the fullness of knowledge that Jesus received, as seen in Luke, was no simple "snap your fingers and you're wise" occurrence.

> *And when he was twelve years old, they went up to Jerusalem after the custom of the feast. And when they had fulfilled the days, as they returned, the child Jesus tarried behind in Jerusalem; and Joseph and his mother knew not of it. But they, supposing him to have been in the company, went a day's journey; and they sought him among their kinsfolk and acquaintance. And when they found him not, they turned back again to Jerusalem, seeking him. And it*

came to pass, that after three days they found
him in the temple, sitting in the midst of the doc-
tors, both hearing them, and asking them ques-
tions. And all that heard him were astonished at
his understanding and answers. And when they
saw him, they were amazed: (Luke 2:42-48a)

Referring back to John's comment in chapter 21 of his gospel, there was so much more that Jesus did that was not included in the Scriptures, we have to assume that there was more to the story waiting to be told. John is specific in saying, *there are also many other things which Jesus did…* (John 21:25), that gives us the direct knowledge that much more happened in Jesus' life that was not mentioned. Is it because we either couldn't comprehend the events, or He didn't want us to know until now? I'm still not implying that the Bible is incomplete. Rather it is exactly what God breathed into men to be written and presented for our understanding and knowledge for the perfecting and education of those who believe in Him. I believe that, just as with any other figure and event in history, there is much more to the story than what is written. It's just like when you read the history and biography of Ulysses S. Grant, you don't read that his old schoolmaster came to the White House, knocked on the doors and walked right in to discuss the issues in the President's life. How do I know that? Because of additional writings that my ancestor, who was Grant's schoolmaster, wrote in his own hand and memoirs. So, with the obvious omission of the Scriptures of nearly thirty years of Jesus' life, we must conclude that He didn't just disappear and then return for three years to minister in the Holy Land. We have to believe that many other events took place that weren't included in the gospels, just as John reflects on, but in time would be revealed for the world to know.

Merriam-Webster's Dictionary defines the word "lost" as follows: "taken away or beyond reach or attainment; no longer visible; hopelessly unattainable" *(ref. 28)*. With that definition as our starting point, we could speculate that God possibly with-held these years from our knowledge and beyond our reach. But the word "lost" can also be applied in a variety of ways. For example, "I was lost, but now I'm found," applies here. The knowledge of many biblical sites were once lost but now found for us to view firsthand. As a Christian, this should be exciting news to us. But what about items that may never be seen by the world, such as these lost documents from Ethiopia? Yes, I have had the opportunity to view historically valuable hidden pages written by John that disclose the time lapse in Jesus' life. We were allowed to photograph those pages, but the world may never actually see these documents on display as you may see the Dead Sea Scrolls exhibition in the Shrine of the Book in the Israel Museum or the Declaration of Independence in Washington D.C.'s National Archives Museum.

Re-examining the Scriptures, this same thought comes to mind regarding the Ark of the Covenant and its whereabouts. The theories of its location are in most cases just that, a theory. From a biblical perspective, we see justification for the Ark's current resting place by looking ahead to the future. At some time in history, the Ark and Mercy Seat will re-emerge to fulfill its purpose with Christ. Looking at the reference as "hopelessly unattainable," we are sure to see that this is simply not the case when it comes to God, the Bible, and anything else to do with it. As we read in Mark 10:27 in Jesus' own words, *With men it is impossible, but not with God: for with God all things are possible*. We simply find that if God is involved, we can't assume that these documents, years, and artifacts are lost. With God, nothing is ever truly lost.

For nearly two thousand years, the trek of the holy family was thought to be a myth or fable. Today, many still think it is. Through nearly two thousand years of hidden secrets about the holy family's trip through Egypt, the documents we were shown weren't lost after all. They had merely been sealed from the rest of the world, documents that would confirm and elaborate on the holy family's journey. The same theory applies to the life of Christ. Somewhere, the story of His untold days on this Earth are safeguarded until the time is right to share them with the world.

Jesus' long and dangerous journey to Ethiopia explains why the holy family continued to travel the Nile River southward to the bottom of Egypt, eventually ending in Lake Tana and more precisely, Tana Kirkos Island. This stressful but divinely appointed journey precluded the events that would shape Jesus' ministry. Their presence on Tana Kirkos Island two thousand years ago paved the way for the historical discoveries today, including the time period Jesus was on the island, the accuracy of the tabernacle, the persons included in the journey, their locations, and that God's preparation of Jesus for the years to come. It was a "crash course" for Jesus in what was to become the greatest ministry in the history of mankind.

When we began our research, we had no idea that such important documents and writings would be revealed to us. I was in search for clues to the whereabouts of the Ark of the Covenant, as well as to reach the people of this country. In turn, God opened up the only evidence of the Ark's existence and then trusted me to uncover the once lost story of a young boy who made a long strenuous journey with His family to arrive at a mysterious island for a biblical meeting beyond comprehension. As the Aba said, this has been a secret of Ethiopia for nearly 2,000 years. As with many artifacts and sites that are being uncovered in and near the Holy Land, the secret of Jesus' meeting with His Father was no longer to be a secret. As it is with everything in God's revelation, it was time for the Heavenly Summit to be revealed to the world. It was time to begin filling in even more of the mystery of Jesus as a boy.

REFERENCE TO ETHIOPIA IN THE BIBLE

Even though the newly discovered information about Ethiopia is overwhelming, biblical and historical texts support the findings. From the Garden of Eden, to Moses' wife, to Jesus in Ethiopia, to the eunuch (or general) of Ethiopia, the evidence and clues that the Bible provides, supported by archeological finds and historical writings, give us overwhelming evidence that Ethiopia plays more importance than what we have been taught over the centuries. However, to defend those who have been teaching, tradition has always focused on the area in and around Jerusalem and not beyond its borders. The entire land mentioned in God's Old Testament should be referenced as the Holy Land. God used it all in many ways for His purpose, and this particular plot of land in the Eastern Central part of Africa was the farthest land to the south that He mentioned in His early Word.

Could Ethiopia have been host to a heavenly summit? Is this the place that God has entrusted to guard the Ark of the Covenant and His Throne? There has to be much more to this story than we may have first realized, and it opens up opportunity for future explorations and revelations.

THE BIBLICAL RECORD

Using the Bible timeline in Luke 2:7, we note the birth of Jesus in Bethlehem, *And she brought forth her firstborn son, and wrapped him in swaddling clothes, and laid him in a manger*, which explains the basis of the journey by Mary and Joseph to the city of Joseph's lineage. The census, as ordered by Caesar Augustus, was probably God's way of getting them to make the trek in the first place. Just as He does in our lives when He needs something accomplished, the Lord will use other means to get us there and then reveal the true need after we have arrived. Following the visit by the shepherds, Jesus was circumcised (Luke 2:21); a few days later Mary and Joseph took Him to Jerusalem to present Him to the Lord, a custom at that time, and it is still a custom in some beliefs today. This young couple stood in wonder as Simeon prophesized their Son's future.

Following this event, and the timeline Matthew chapter two tells about, the wise men traveled to Jerusalem. King Herod learned of their journey, and their purpose to follow the star that was leading them to worship the King of the Jews;

> *Then Herod, when he had privily called the wise men, inquired of them diligently what time the star appeared. And he sent them to Bethlehem, and said, Go and search diligently for the young child; and when ye have found him, bring me word again, that I may come and worship him also. When they had heard the king, they departed; and, lo, the star, which they saw in the east, went before them, till it came and stood over where the young child was. When they saw the star, they rejoiced with exceeding great joy.* (Matthew 2:7-10)

As we know, there was more to Herod's bidding than to worship Jesus. He played the wise men as pawns in order to find the location of Jesus, who was a threat to his reign as king, but God redirected them not to return to Jerusalem because of Herod's ulterior motive (Matthew 2:12). We also learn in this portion of Matthew that when the wise men arrived in the house (an obvious move from a stable) they worshipped a young boy, not the small baby as seen in Luke chapter two:

> *And when they were come into the house, they*
> *saw the young child with Mary his mother, and*
> *fell down, and worshipped him: and when they*
> *had opened their treasures, they presented unto*
> *him gifts; gold, and frankincense, and myrrh...*
> (Matthew 2:11)

From this point, with Herod's pending decree to have all the young children two and under killed, we must assume that Jesus was around the age of two at this time. It was here that Joseph receives a visit by an angel:

> *And when they were departed, behold, the angel*
> *of the Lord appeareth to Joseph in a dream,*
> *saying, Arise, and take the young child and his*
> *mother, and flee into Egypt, and be thou there*
> *until I bring thee word: for Herod will seek the*
> *young child to destroy him. When he arose, he*
> *took the young child and his mother by night,*
> *and departed into Egypt...* (Matthew 2:13, 14)

This is where events become vague and speculative. From around the age of two, presumably, until the approximate age of twelve, we are lost in the world of speculation to the whereabouts and activities of Jesus and His family. Or at least that has been the thought for nearly 1,900 years. Just as we must look into historical records and recorded eyewitness accounts of some of the most popular figures in history, we must do the same for the miracle- filled life of Jesus Christ, otherwise we simply make Him unbelievable. We know they went into Egypt, so that was the perfect place to look for clues about their trek throughout that country. Although some of the recorded events may appear exaggerated, we have to remember that we are talking about Jesus, the Messiah, and that anything is possible through God.

We now return our attention to the oral and written historic text in the Egyptian accounts, and the Coptic biblical historic record and hidden Muslim record to make sense of the southward journey of the holy family through Egypt and then farther down the Nile River to Ethiopia in Lake Tana. They finally arrive on Tana Kirkos Island, where Jesus met with God Himself. With the documented writings hidden on the island of Tana Kirkos, recited by Mary and Salome, and recorded by the Apostle John with Prochorus as the penman who then delivered them to the Ethiopians for secret storage, we can see God's accuracy and timetable beginning to take shape. After Jesus grew in wisdom and understanding, the holy family made their way back to Egypt and took up shelter in Al Murharraq awaiting the call to return home. Scripture tells us that an angel came to Joseph in much the same way as when he was told to go into Egypt:

> *But when Herod was dead, behold, an angel*
> *of the Lord appeareth in a dream to Joseph in*
> *Egypt, Saying, Arise, and take the young child*
> *and his mother, and go into the land of Israel:*
> *for they are dead which sought the young child's*

> *life. And he arose, and took the young child and*
> *his mother, and came into the land of Israel.*
> *But when he heard that Archelaus did reign in*
> *Judaea in the room of his father Herod, he was*
> *afraid to go thither: notwithstanding, being*
> *warned of God in a dream, he turned aside into*
> *the parts of Galilee: And he came and dwelt in*
> *a city called Nazareth: that it might be fulfilled*
> *which was spoken by the prophets, He shall be*
> *called a Nazarene.* (Matthew 2:19-23)

In these five verses, we see Joseph's encounter with the angel once again giving him the all clear to return to Israel. But he was apprehensive about Jerusalem, however, because Archelaus, Herod's son, was now the reigning king. So, Joseph packed up his family and traveled back into Israel, bypassing Jerusalem and traveling into Galilee, back to their new home in Nazareth. This agrees with Luke 2:39, *And when they had performed all things according to the law of the Lord, they returned into Galilee, to their own city Nazareth.*

This recorded return to Nazareth confirms my own thoughts, specifically noted while sitting on a rock outside the ancient treasury on Tana Kirkos Island.

> *And the child grew, and waxed strong in spirit,*
> *filled with wisdom: and the grace of God was*
> *upon him.* (Luke 2:40)

The holy family had to take this detour for Jesus to receive His strong spirit and wisdom. After their return to Israel, the young Jesus astonished some of Jerusalem's most educated men with His Spirit-filled conversation.

> *And it came to pass, that after three days they found him in the temple, sitting in the midst of the doctors, both hearing them, and asking them questions. And all that heard him were astonished at his understanding and answers.* (Luke 2:46,47)

At the age of twelve, we know He confounded those who were in His presence. Some eighteen years later, He did the same when He appeared to the world as the Son of God, the Savior, the Lord of Lords, and the King of Kings. Wouldn't we like to know about those interim years not mentioned in the gospels? I believe it's only a matter of time before God reveals those to us. Even the Ethiopians who guard this sacred evidence do not understand the extent of their Holy treasury.

SO...WHAT'S NEXT?

When we really step back and examine the whole picture about the next piece of the biblical puzzle to be unearthed, we must first allow our hearts and minds to be opened to anything. In the last ten years, we have seen a mounting list of historical finds that line up with events in the Bible, such as the anchors from the Apostle Paul's shipwreck; the etchings confirming the existence of the House of David; various writings and scrolls uncovering of the Siloam Pool; the continued research on the locations of Sodom and Gomorrah; the finding of the ancient boat in the Sea of Galilee; evidence to the true site of Mount Sinai and the split rock; the church of Mary Magdalene; the location of Herod's tomb; and hundreds of other confirmations that are becoming truly overwhelming, but each amazing in their own right. The discoveries are coming so quickly that publications can't keep up with them.

So, what is next. I truly believe that the doors have been unlocked to what God will allow to be found. Just as we stumbled upon these historic and revealing pages of Jesus' early life and the discovery of the footholds of the Ark, the same is true with the future unearthing of what only God knows will be next. What I think is more important is that we keep our minds open to the new discoveries and let our discernment help us to find the truth along the way, not what man believes and teaches, but what God will reveal to the history of His creation and His Son. I prayed diligently about the authenticity of this information. I spent hours upon hours in solitude and prayer deliberating over the findings and the documents that we were shown. After putting all of the evidence on paper, God then opened up the path and threw bread crumbs along the trail for me to either deny or to pick up and move forward.

This has truly been an interesting journey, one of unsuspecting revelation and struggle. No doubt there will be some who question our evidence and rightfully so. I was one of those who doubted. But as I have heard many say before, until you have been there, felt the hand of God on the journey, seen doors opened to clear the path, and felt the joy that comes when following His lead, then I encourage you to at least consider the worthiness of the evidence. Just as I had doubted the opportunity of salvation through Jesus Christ, I am truly joyful that I opened up my eyes and my heart to His eternal assurance. My only regret is that I didn't do that earlier in my life. I pray this analogy enlightens your understanding.

In the Holy Bible in the book of Luke, Jesus sat with His disciples and many others who gathered with them, and He began to share a parable about the sower of the seed. This popular parable pinpoints where our faith lies, and it is the foundation of the truth that our roots are secured in. When Jesus came to the end of the parable, He gave the answer to understanding the mysteries that the Bible holds, and foretold the mysteries that are still to come:

> *And he said, Unto you it is given to know the mysteries of the kingdom of God: but to others in parables; that seeing they might not see, and hearing they might not understand. Now the parable is this: The seed is the word of God.*
> (Luke 8:10, 11)

In this passage, Jesus tells us that those who truly believe in Him and fill themselves with the knowledge and Word of God and His teachings will have a better understanding in His revelation of the mysteries of the Lord. But those who don't

275

believe in Him will have a great deal of trouble understanding and believing. God's Word lays the foundation, and trusting in Him will open up the doors to a greater and fulfilled understanding. I sometimes wonder what I missed during my years of struggling with the truths and not putting my faith in God's Word. It's as simple as this: trust in Him and the rest will surely come in abundance.

In many cases, we find that these holy sites and newly discovered biblical un-coverings have long been revered by those living in their proximity, and they have been paying homage to these sites, or secrets, for centuries. Just as the truth of Jesus' arrival in Ethiopia has been revealed in this book, so has this secret been guarded by the Ethiopians for thousands of years until now. God had chosen their land to house His secrets only to be revealed in His timeline. Were the years of Jesus as a boy and those after His encounter in the temple teaching really lost? I would have to say no, they aren't really lost, but they are simply hidden away until the appointed time where God feels that we are ready for the next revelation. So, what's next? That is a question that only the Lord can answer, but when it is revealed to us, one thing is for sure; it will be spectacular and aligned with every truth He has ever given us.

Chapter 15:

AN ADVENTURE OF A LIFETIME BEGINS

IT ALL STARTED WITH a phone call and ended up with a discovery of the only evidence known to the Ark of the Covenant's existence and the revelation of a lost story about what truly happened to Jesus as a boy. We know the Bible only mentions that the holy family was told to go to Egypt, but through a tremendous amount of research and a miraculous experience, we now know that the journey of this young boy, who would one day save the world, was much more than a retreat. During this adventure, I discovered my skepticism, a critic to anything that was out of the traditional box. Then I looked at my own life, and realized that I was far from the tradition. I was raised a Catholic, saved a Pentecostal, and baptized a Baptist. I have studied hundreds of hours to achieve a Doctorite in Theology, and spent incredible hours in archeological training both in books and field form, but nothing had prepared me for what was to come. Yet, I was over my head in the tradition of man in the church. I was told "if we don't teach it and the Bible don't state it, then it ain't true." Then Abraham Lincoln wasn't our sixteenth president, I guess. Now I have realized how ridiculous that really is. With a statement like that, we start to realize how so many people today can't get a grasp on the Christian faith. We start to realize that statements like that bring no credit to God or the teachings of Jesus. Anyone blind enough to overlook the fact that we have nearly thirty years of the life of Christ untold in the Bible and believe that absolutely nothing happened worth telling during those years has just compromised the power of our Lord and Savior.

I don't believe in compromising the Word of God in any way. At the same time, I don't believe that we must dismiss the obvious when God is calling us into another direction or journey in our lives. Many believers miss the opportunities and blessings that God bestows on them because their short minded, traditional theories and beliefs hampered them from seeing the truth before them. When God opens the gates, and sweeps the walkway for us to run the race, as the Apostle Paul referred to in Hebrews 12:1b-2a, *let us lay aside every weight, and the sin which doth so easily beset us, and let us run with patience the race that is set before us, Looking unto Jesus the author and finisher of our faith*, then we are to follow that path until the mission of the Lord is completed. Sometimes we are not privileged to know the outcome in the beginning, but when our eyes are opened, we will see the glory of His will for the adventure in the end. And then there are times where we may never know why He sends us on a pathway in our lives.

This adventure to a forbidden island, to a people scattered and peeled, to a land of beauty and a land of pain, was set before us, and God Himself swept the path clean for us to complete the journey. Now that we have completed this portion of the mission, you begin to see a clearer picture that there is much more to come. Much more to be revealed in time, and it will all come in "such a time as this."

A RETURN TO THE BEGINNING

An opportunity arose for Sherri and I to return to the Smoky Mountain area where all of this journey began with the dream in the middle of the night. We had a speaking engagement at a church in Pigeon Forge, Tennessee, and decided to revisit some of the places where this journey began. So early the next morning after we had arrived, Sherri and I had breakfast, and then drove off to Gatlinburg. We passed the hotel where I had the dream and Sherri said, "There's where all this began." We looked up as we drove by, and turned and looked at each other with a smile on our faces. It was a reflection of thankfulness for what God has entrusted us with.

We then turned up a side-street, and made a left down the parkway to Route 321, turned right and began our drive up to the craftsman area in the Smoky Mountains. We made a left down the side-road where a few years earlier we had made a trip to a conglomerate of little shops where the woman put the hammered silver trumpets necklace around my neck on that faithful day of revelation. We pulled in, and the place was completely uninhabited. I mean, this place looked like nothing had been there for years. Sherri and I looked at each other bewildered that nothing was there. Not one shop was occupied, almost like nothing was ever there.

Confused, we turned around and took a back road to get to Pigeon Forge to revisit Mr. Williams shop in the Old Mill area. Sherri went off to a pottery shop; I had my manuscript, and headed over to his shop. He was inside at the counter working on a project, and we exchanged hellos and a handshake. I reminded him of the day that I was there, but didn't reflect on the events that had happened. I simply opened the manuscript to the events I shared with you earlier in the book (chapter 2), and handed it to him to read. He began to read it, and I could see the look on his face change. He finished, and looked up to me and said, "Jim, I don't know what to say." His eyes teared up and what he said left me speechless, "Jim, I've never had a woman like that working in here. That was not of this place." He was reflecting that this was not someone working here, but something in the form of a woman that took me to that painting of the Ark of the Covenant. He shook my hand, turned his head side to side in disbelief, and walked into the room behind his register. I knew he was touched, as was I in what was revealed. I know I shared these events earlier, but it is well-worth revisiting to show how God orchestrates our paths. God had set this up, and it was God that continued to amaze all along this journey. It's just like a beautiful symphony and God is the conductor. We are the musicians that play and reflect the breathtaking music that God has orchestrated to the world. When we don't take our seat with our instrument is when the world falls into confusion. I, though, intend on playing the instrument that God has given me to my very best ability, even though it's not what man really wants to hear in this day and age.

A TIMELINE OF UNDERSTANDING

The pieces of the puzzle have now been filled in. The discoveries and all of the evidence has been laid out. Now let's look at the timeline so everything is understood where it falls in God's perfect timing. There's no doubt that God dropped the bread crumbs in the pathway for us; thus, when you look at this timeline, you see His hand lead every path of this adventure.

1) *In the beginning, God created...* (Genesis 1:1). These words begin everything in God's view, and that's where we start our quest of understanding.

2) God calls Moses on Mt. Sinai to build the Ark and the Throne that He will meet upon, and to place it in the tabernacle. Aaron, Moses' brother will be the high priest, and it will be guarded by the tribe of the Levites. (Exodus 25:10-22)

3) During the reign of Manasseh and his defilement of the holy temple is the most likely time the Ark of the Covenant would have been removed for safety and purity.

4) King Josiah, Manasseh's grandson, cries out to the Levites in 2 Chronicles 35:3 to return the holy Ark to Israel.

5) Upon Josiah's threat against Pharaoh Necho of Egypt as he passes by Israel with his army to battle Carchemish near the Euphrates, we see that the Pharaoh has the Ark in his possession as he refers to getting his commands from God, who must be speaking to the Levitical high priest in his country (2 Chronicles 20-22).

6) At this same time in Egypt, a temple measuring nearly the size of Solomon's Temple was built on Elephantine Island in the Aswan Valley in the southern portion of Egypt on the Nile River where the Levites were holding sacrificial ceremonies within the Holy of Holies.

7) 410 B.C., the temple was destroyed on Elephantine Island, but the Levites disappeared with no loss of life, and all treasures of the temple were removed and taken with them.

8) The Ark was then moved south to the source of the Nile River, Lake Tana, Ethiopia, and placed on a stone platform on Tana Kirkos Island, a Holy of Holies was built around, and the Levites continued the Atonement ceremonies on the island.

9) The prophet Isaiah states in chapter 7:14-16 that the coming Messiah will be somewhat weaned into knowing what He will be sent to do.

10) Isaiah, in chapter 18, tells us that the country of Ethiopia will be returning the holy Throne to Jesus in the Holy of Holies.

11) The prophet Zephaniah tells us in Chapter 3:10 again that the Ethiopians will be returning the *gift* to Jesus in a celebrated event.

12) Jesus, the Messiah, is born in Bethlehem in Luke 2.

13) Matthew's gospel informs us that wise men saw the star that lead them to find the newborn King. King Herod tries to convince these men to come back and tell him where the child was located because he wanted to worship Him as well. This was an obvious lie, and God gave the wise men discernment not to tell him. The wise men came to Jesus, who is now a child living in a home and must have been near the age of two at the time. They worship Him, present gifts, and depart, not returning to tell Herod of His whereabouts (Matthew 2:1-12).

14) In anger, Herod orders that all the male children under the age of two in his kingdom should be killed to protect against this King (Matthew 2:16).

15) Joseph receives the call from an angel to take Jesus, Mary, and himself, and retreat into Egypt, and God will inform them when to return, leading to ten of the missing years from the canonical Bible (Matthew 2:13).

16) A documented history has been located that describes the next several years in Jesus' life, and His family's life as they traveled through Egypt along the Nile River, including a stop in Sakha, where Jesus, the boy, left the impression of His foot in stone. Then it was discovered that the family stopped in the far south of Egypt and stayed in Al Murharraq.

17) Ancient historical accounts report that Jesus, Mary, and Salome (John's mother and wife of Zebedee) are rowed with two oarsmen on a papyrus boat to Tana Kirkos. Joseph stays on the mainland to work for money for the return trip home.

18) For three months and ten days, Jesus goes daily to meet with Father God at the Throne upon the Ark of the Covenant, to be educated on the grace, wisdom, and knowledge that is described in Isaiah 7:14-16 and fulfilled in Luke 2:40.

19) Upon Jesus' completion, He climbs to the top of the cliff, where His mother had prayed daily for Him, and embedded His footprint distinctly in the stone upon the cliff.

20) They return to Al Muharraq, and Joseph received the calling from the angel to return home (Matthew 2:19-23).

21) Jesus returns and astonishes the men in the temple in Jerusalem with His knowledge at the age of twelve (Luke 2:42-48). Following this event, we don't see Jesus again until He's thirty years of age.

22) Jesus begins His ministry, and at the age of thirty-three, He is arrested, mocked, beaten, and made to carry His cross to Golgotha to be crucified as found in the four gospels. Golgotha is said to be, in Matthew 27:33, *the place of a skull.*

23) Jesus gasps for a breath, and cries out to God and says, *"It is finished,"* and then takes His final breath. Upon His death on the cross, the Earth shakes with a great

earthquake, and the temple veil is ripped from the top to bottom, opening the door for those who believe in Jesus to have direct access to Him. The rocks also begin to break apart.

24) On Tana Kirkos Island, the platform in which the Throne (Mercy Seat) and the Ark of the Covenant are sitting, cracks and shifts the center holes of the footholds of the Ark. The two eastern pole holes break off and fall into the waters below.

25) Jesus returns after the third day and leaves the tomb He was sealed in and begins teaching and preparing the apostles for a life of ministry. As He stands to prepare for His ascension into Heaven, Jesus once again leaves the impressions of His feet in the stone.

26) Queen Candice of Ethiopia sends her general (the eunuch), the keeper of her treasury, which would have included the Ark and Throne, to Jerusalem to see if it was possibly time to return the Throne. In the confusion of not finding the Messiah (who had ascended) he is approached by Phillip and is lead to Christ and baptized in the water nearby.

27) Prochorus scribes the book for John describing the story of Jesus' travels to Ethiopia, which is given to him from his mother Salome and Jesus' mother Mary, as John was told by Jesus on the cross to take care of her. This is the reason John added the final thought to his gospel telling us that Jesus had done so much more that wasn't

written in the Scriptures (John 21:25). Prochorus then scribes the book of Revelation for John on Patmos.

28) 310 A.D., King Ezana takes the Ark of the Covenant to Axum, Ethiopia in which still today a Guardian keeps watch, along with armed gunmen, over the Ark and the Throne in the St. Mary of Zion Church. Next to the church are also the ancient hammered trumpets of Moses (Numbers 10) mentioned in Isaiah 18, that will be blown when they return the Throne to Jesus to the Holy of Holies in the new temple.

29) Sometime between 615-622 A.D., Muhammad declares an act of peace forevermore with Ethiopia because of a gesture of agreement with the Axumite King during the migration period. Muhammad agreed to a protection over Ethiopia from agreession and writes the account into the Book of Battles in the Quran.

30) Ethiopia begins a process of protecting their God given treasures through a variety of traditions, and the world turns away in disbelief to keep them safe until the time He begins to reveal them to the world.

31) On Tana Kirkos Island still today, the implements used in the sacrificial ceremony on the Day of Atonement, are housed in the treasury from the days prior to Jesus going to the cross.

32) Today we are still waiting on the blowing of the trumpets and the sign in the mountains as the Ethiopians are planning for the return of the Throne to Jesus in Jerusalem!

33) The time has arrived as the Lord opens up the mysteries through the truth and puts aside the tradition. It's time for the world to know.

A RETURN VISIT TO THE TREASURY

Over the next couple of years, I made many trips back to Ethiopia for research, exploration, and ministry work. Upon one journey back to Axum, Sisay met me at the airport and said that he didn't know that it was me that he was meeting. Many times, I don't announce my coming, so I don't get mixed up into unplanned meetings but can get right to work. Sisay said, "I want to take you to the treasury of the Ark. I have something I must show you."

We made our way from the airport to our old motel upon the cliff-side, dropped off luggage and grabbed a soft drink just to take a break. Tim Moore had made the trip with me, and we knew that God had something planned for us this time. The van pulled up and took us down to the treasury building next to the St. Mary of Zion church. We made our way down and removed everything that was electronic from my person. They don't allow anything that could possibly record or take pictures inside the treasury.

Jim and Sisay at the lower courtyard of the St. Mary of Zion Church, the
location of the Ark of the Covenant today, in Axum, Ethiopia.

Sisay was anxious, but didn't want to show any excitement, as he normally does when it comes to a new revealing
of something. We walked to the shelves to the right-side of the
room, that are now enclosed in glass. Inside are the crowns of
the kings that I mentioned in my first visit, along with many
artifacts, most of which are made of solid gold. As we looked at
one of the engraved objects in the treasury, Sisay had continued
to search for anything to do with the Ark, and somehow, he
got a glimpse of this object and had to show me. Pointing into

the case at a gold panel, on the side was a clear engraving of the Ark of the Covenant. The Ethiopians don't have trinkets or paintings of the Ark of the Covenant or the Mercy Seat because of the reverence of these objects to them in the presence of God.

As Sisay pointed this out, it took a minute to realize what he was trying to show me. Then it became extremely clear. The engraving was clearly the Ark and the Mercy Seat, with rays of light shining from it. It was amazing, and the first actual picture, or engraving, I have seen of the holy object here. What's even more amazing, this etching appeared to depict exactly what most agree the Ark looked like. It was very similar to the most common versions depicted in the movies and old etchings in older Bibles and ancient books. This was a great find, and one that I'm thankful my friend Sisay was able to find for me.

CONFIRMING THE PATH

It's funny sometimes to see how God confirms your path. I strongly feel we lose so many blessings in our lives because we refuse to open our eyes and see the Lord work in us. I would like to share one quick example of how God continually confirms what He has laid before you. Months after returning from Ethiopia, the week had arrived for me to gather our team together, and head down to the Bible publishing company to print the Ethiopian Amharic translations of the Bible for our return trip in January of the next year. Monday started off hectic, as always, with the basic chaos of getting the week ready for the numerous activities ahead. I had plopped into my seat in my office to finalize the covers for the Bibles from the photos that I had taken during our journey. A gentleman at the Bearing Precious Seed Bible Publishing Company had been working on the covers for a couple of weeks and was now waiting on my approval to finalize the project. They looked great, and I sat in tears staring at the sample on my computer screen. To think that just months earlier I thought that I was heading out to search for trail of the Ark of the Covenant, and now I'm writing a book and preparing to return to share the gospel with these wonderful people and to continue my research.

Tuesday was somewhat different. I had made my final calls to our team to remind them of Saturday's gathering to print and prepare the Bibles while also carrying out a variety of other duties I needed to accomplish. Back in January I had put together a plan for a Bible study group that I also teach on Tuesday nights. Remember, this was planned in January, and we are now talking the end of August. When I pulled up the study that I had prepared, which was the book of Acts that we had been on for several weeks with a couple of chapters that we were coming back to for further study, I realized that our final chapter was to go over, in more detail, Acts chapter eight with Phillip and his encounter with the Ethiopian Eunuch. My first thought was how fitting, we are going to print the Ethiopian Bibles on Saturday, and today we just so happen to be con-cluding our study of Acts and returning to chapter eight, as I had preset the first week of the year.

The study was amazing, as I had a whole new perspec-tive on why this man was in Jerusalem, and now in the desert, puzzled by what he was attempting to read in the book of Isaiah. Bible study ended around eight o'clock this night, and Sherri and I went home to prepare ourselves for a good night's sleep. At ten I went up to our room and was about ready to shut off the lights when my phone rang. On the other end of the line was my good friend Yonas, the Ethiopian who helped translate the ancient book with priest in Cincinnati at the public library. He said, "Jim, do you remember I invite you to a celebration at our church when we meet?" I replied, "Of course, I remember." Actually, I had forgotten about it until he mentioned it, and I just figured that it had already passed. He said, "I would like to ask you to come with your wife this Saturday to our church in Cincinnati in the morning." I was somewhat disappointed at first because I realized that we had to print the Bibles this Saturday morning. I regretfully told Yonas about our conflict and that we had to be there at nine in the morning. But he responded, again, with that assuring and bubbly Ethiopian response, "No problem!" He went on to say, "Our celebration and services begin at three thirty in the morning and you can come and be with us." I quickly said, "Three thirty in the morning, are you kidding me?" Yonas, thinking I was kidding said, "Yes, Jim, and we will continue until after noon. You can come be with us?"

I knew that I had been given the honor of being asked to attend this service, and that it was the least I could do for what they both had done for me. I quickly said, "We will be there. Can I bring others with me?" He came back with what I expected, "Of course, you can. I see you Saturday morning!"

He was excited, and admittedly, I was too. It just hit me like a ton of bricks what was going on here. It was God's sign to me that He was confirming all that has, and is about to happen regarding this journey.

Saturday arrived and the stars were bright in the early morning sky as we started out for our journey to the church in Cincinnati. We met up with three others, as we loaded up and headed to the downtown services. I really had no idea where this place was, and I gave all my hope to the GPS to make sure we arrived in the correct location. As I thought from my discussion at the library, this church was in the downtown area, but much to my surprise it was in the rougher area in Cincinnati. As we drove, we came to a somewhat broken-down location, but the GPS had us turn down a dark alley. I was beginning to wonder what I had gotten us into. But somehow, I knew that God was behind all of this, so there was nothing to worry about.

We drove through the alley where there were three older buildings on the right and some homes that had seen better days on the left. I didn't see anything that reminded me of a church, or anything moving around, as if a church service was going on. So, I drove our van out and went back around, turning back into the alley, for another pass. This time I rolled the windows down on both sides so I could listen. Then I heard it. Pounding slow rhythms on a large drum brought back the memories of the ceremony at Timkat in Axum, as well as the bass pounding drum in the temple on Tana Kirkos Island. I pulled to the front of an old building with some type of covering over the door, as we could barely see a speck of light shining through a tear in the covering. And then my hunch came true when I heard a loud call, "Lilililililililililili." This is the Ethiopian call in unison that we heard through the night at a wedding ceremony near the Stelae Park and at various other times while in Axum. I exclaimed, "We're in the right place."

We parked in a small parking spot between two buildings and made our way in. Yonas just happened to be at the front door. He was thrilled we had made it. He had to step out for something, so he made sure the others were aware we were there, and they were instructed to help us in anything we needed. We removed our shoes before entering the sanctuary, and I noticed on the wall banners depicting Axum and Gondar. Most of the people, before entering the sanctuary would get down on their knees and bow low to kiss the floor out of respect, based on the orthodox custom. The men and women were all wrapped in prayer shawls, with the woman and children were on the right side of the isle, and the men on the left. In the front was the Aba, along with the musicians on the drums and deacons, or monks, holding their prayer sticks. They were in unison, with a flick of the wrist, playing their sistrum, a silver or tin instrument likened to a hand-held combination of a small cymbal and castanet.

As we took our seats and watched, I couldn't help but wander back to Axum. My mind was flashing faces and places from this humble setting nearly eight thousand miles away. The Aba handed his prayer stick to another man as he took a break from the service. As he walked down the aisle, I made my way into the foyer of the church. He glanced once, and then took a double take when he saw my face. With a smile, he gave a slight bow, as did I, and we exchanged the traditional Ethiopian handshake, and went side to side toward each other in a show of respect. It was a comforting feeling, like I was at home with them.

We watched them worship hour by hour, with chants of prayers and Scripture from their Bibles. Each word seemed to coordinate with the slow beat of the music. Occasionally others would make their way into the sanctuary, but at no time did anyone look at us any differently. Once in a while, the same as in Axum, the drum beat would quicken and the Aba, along with the others of dignity in the front, would hit their prayer sticks on the floor while moving in closer to each other. Just as the prayer sticks would hit the floor, the women would again give a loud burst of "Lilililililililililili." It was amazing, and was almost like a welcome home to the land of Ethiopia.

My watch ticked up to eight in the morning, and it was time for us to go. I had one of the men go to the front and tell Yonas to meet me in the foyer of the church. We shook hands and he leaned over to me and said, "Jim, remember, here you are always with friends." It brought tears to my eyes as I was reminded of the friendship and warmth of the people of Ethiopia. Upon returning from Ethiopia, I had Larry Stinson, my jeweler friend from Tennessee, design some very unique pendants of the trumpets that we were honored to see from Moses in Axum's treasury. I reached into my pocket and grabbed a double silver trumpet pendant and gave it to Yonas as a gift of continued friendship. Tears began to show in his eyes as he nodded, as if to say, "Thank you." We shook hands once more, and as I turned for the door, the Aba was standing there. He reached for my hand, and we both gave a slight bow in respect to each other. I told him I had to go, and Jonas began to explain why we were unable to stay further into the service. It was an awesome experience, to relive the faithfulness of the Ethiopian people. But for now, it was time to go. We scurried to the van and loaded up, and I realized the importance of this relationship and how God directed us together.

We made it back to our church just in time to load everyone up and head to the Bible publishing building. Thirty people had gathered to help, and the strong smell of incense was permeating from our clothes from the church service we had just attended as we entered into the van. Everyone was in a great mood, and Sherri and I, and the others who traveled earlier with us were already on fire to get to work on the Bibles since our unforgettable early morning encounter. Before entering the publishing building, we all bowed our heads in prayer in the hopes that these Bibles will reach people all around the world. They say that the average Bible will be read by seven people. That figure gives me great hope to know that thousands will have their hands on these books, and also that thousands more will be touched by what we are about to do.

The pages had been printed and the covers were ready to go. Our crew had to first assemble the Scripture in order and then put the appropriate covers over them. Since the pages were rough cuts, they had to be tapped down to get them as close to flush at the top as possible. With that complete we began to staple them together while others took the completed books by tens in an alternating manner. Then, five hundred or so at a time, we wheeled them out to others in our group, and they ran them through the cutter to make them into perfect Scriptures, ready to box and take with us. I had pulled the first ones out of the stack to complete a particular project that Sherri had reminded me to do. Back in 2001, on a mission's trip into Mexico, Dr. Verlis Collins, once a missionary for this publishing company, was driving the bus that took our group into the country. As we drove for nearly eight hours through the Mexican desert, he shared his story about how people all over the world have their fingerprints on our lives. He said that someone led the preacher that shared the gospel of Christ with me to lead me to the Lord. So now, their fingerprints were on me. And that continues on and on. I had always remembered that from Mr. Collins. That always rang true for me anytime I had an opportunity to witness to anyone. I had brought a stamp pad with me and had all those involved stamp their fingerprints on the cover of this Bible. I framed it as a memento of the day, and as a reminder of our fingerprints on the world.

THE FINAL TOUCH

I learned a great deal while standing on the cliffs in Axum and Tana Kirkos, gazing into a vast desert or over the massive lake alone with God. I'm a different person today because of what I have been shown, trusted with, and witnessed as God cleared a path. He presented me with an opportunity of a different sort in order to get my attention. He stopped me in my tracks and took away what pride I had to make me listen. He introduced me to a loving, humble, praying group of selfless people, to show me how to trust only in Him, as they do. Then, when all was in order, He brought me to my knees-twice-to share a story about a meeting that took place long, long ago in a land far, far away from home. First, to call me with His trumpets to share a story with others, to show how these trumpets will symbolize the calling out of His story to the world. Then to my knees on a cliffside on an island shrouded in mystery and intrigue, to give me the hidden journey of His Son and the meeting on an island flowing with righteousness. Even after I returned home, He continued to open doors and lay the crumbs along the path to finish His wish. I'm very different today than I was prior to this adventure. If anything is true, I have learned to trust in God to direct my paths in every way. If He is calling you to a place in your life, it's to your benefit to listen.

> *In all thy ways acknowledge him, and he shall direct thy paths.* (Proverbs 3:6)

I have learned through this adventure how true Solomon's wisdom really is. If we allow God to direct our paths, then we really have so much more opened to us during our journeys through life.

Dr. Jim and Sherri Rankin standing high above the
Great Rift Valley in Ethiopia.

The words that my wife Sherri said to me just three days
before we were invited to become part of this exploration have
come true over and over again. I came away from this journey
with a love and passion to help the people of Ethiopia and to
share their need with others in a different sort of adventure. In
the process of it all, God allowed me the privilege of uncovering one of His most hidden secrets, a revelation about His
meeting with His only begotten Son on a remote island that was
completely removed from the world.

This revelation of the mighty summit of God passing on
to Jesus the knowledge, power, and grace to prepare Him for
the greatest ministry ever, may be one of the most revealing
finds in recent years. For you and me, this information puts an
important piece in the puzzle to the missing years in the life of

Jesus Christ and clarifies the one line of Scripture in Luke 2 to open our eyes to answer where and when Jesus received the wisdom and grace He carried with Him. It also gave us physical proof that the Ark of the Covenant and God's Throne, the Mercy Seat, was truly a real object, which our faith confirms, with my discovery of the footholds on the island. Although stepping back and looking at the whole picture now, I know that is only the beginning of our journeys through life. God allows us to travel through many valleys in our lives in order to prepare us for the great blessings that are still to come. In this adventure, it is evident to me that we have the opportunity to make great friends through our continued travels to Ethiopia, and that there is much more work to do. While I was speaking in the Dayton, Ohio area, Sherri and I took some time to visit the Wright Brothers bicycle shop and museums. We turned the corner in one of the exhibits and directly in front of us was a huge picture of Orville Wright working on their plane, along with a quote from him that left me in tears. Wright said, "Isn't it astonishing that all these secrets have been preserved for so many years just so that we could discover them!!" I believe that should be truth in our lives, as well. I never, in my wildest dreams, set out to make a discovery such as this. But it was laid out by God, and preserved by Him, until the time that He saw fit to drop me to my knees to discovery this lost secret. We all need to just let God take the wheel and the control, because He has much to reveal to us all.

The excitement builds each time we begin planning for the next journey to this remote land in Africa. Knowing that our fingerprints are on those Scriptures that people will be reading and consequently giving their lives to Christ is reward enough for all the effort and preparation each time we journey there. It's also a thrill to know that God has so much more to reveal in this ancient land, and I can't help but believe that He will open more revelation to us with each and every journey there. But yet, in many more ways, I still see the words that Sherri spoke becoming even more true in the time still ahead: "Jim, I really feel that our biggest and best adventures are still to come."

**"When the trumpets sound...
Arise, and go!"**

Reference Notes:

1. The Holy Bible, King James Version (Referenced Throughout)
2. Penny Caldwell, *God Of The Mountain: True Story Behind The Discoveries At The Real Mount Sinai* (Bridge-Logos Publishers) 2008.
3. Robert Cornuke, *The Relic Quest* (Tyndale House Publishers, Inc.) 2005.
4. Answer In Genesis, *Uncovering The Real Nativity*, 2011
5. Dr. Zahi A. Hawass, *The Magic and Mystery of the Pyramids And the Route of the Holy Family,* (Director of the Pyramids at Giza)
6. Jenny Jobbins, *Jesus in Egypt* (Al-Ahram Weekly) 2001
7. Henry Sike, *First Gospel of the Infancy of Jesus Christ – First Translation*, 1697
8. Paul Perry, *Jesus In Egypt* (Random House Publishing Group, A Ballatine Book) 2003
9. Fr. Philopos Anba–Bishoy, *The Flight of the Holy Family to Egypt*, (Nubar Printing)
10. Nevine Isaak, *Christianity In Egypt*, (RIT Institute), 2013

11. Professor Sergew Habele Selassie, *The Church of Ethiopia A Panorama of History and Spiritual Life* (EOTC Printing), 2003

12. Selamta, *The Legend of Lalibela*, Selamta Publication, October 2016

13. Richard K. P. Pankhurst, *History of Ethiopian Towns: From the Middle Ages to the Early Nineteenth Century*, (Wiesbaden: Franz Steiner Verlag), 1982, vol. 1, pp. 117

14. Julio Etchart, *Where Gods Reposed and Poets Marveled*, (Travel Magazine)

15. Jerry W. Bird, *Bahir Dar, Lake Tana, Blue Nile Falls*, (Africa Magazine), 2010

16. Meera Lester, *Salome, Wife of Zebedee*, (Adams Media), 2009, pp. 150

17. Richard Saunders, *Angelographia*, (London), 1692

18. J.P. Kirsch, *Seven Deacons*, (New York, Robert Appleton Co.), 1912

19. John Able MD, *Beyond Malignant Materialism*, (J.A. Books), 2010

20. *Byzantine Illumination Bible*, (Scribe Unknown), 1100

21. Ayele Bekeri, *St. Yared: The Great Ethiopian Composer*, (Tadias Magazine), 2007

22. Richard A. Lobban, *Historical Dictionary of Ancient and Midieval Nubia*, (Scarecrow Press), 2004, p. 97

23. Miriam Ma'at-ka-re Monges, "Kush", *Encyclopedia of Black Studies*, (Sage Publications), 2005, p. 301-303

24. John Fage, *A History of Africa*, (Routledge), 2015, p. 115

25. Marg Mowczko, *Queen Candace of Ethiopia*, (New Life), 2015

26. David E. Jones, *Women Warriors: A History*, (Brassey's), 2000

27. Flavius Josephus as translated by William Whiston, *The Complete Works: The Jewish War* (Kregel Publications), 1867, 1960

28. Various, Merriam-Webster's Collegiate Dictionary, Merriam-Webster, Inc., 1828-2008

Film References:

'Raiders of the Lost Ark', *Indiana Jones*, George Lucas, LucasFilm, Paramount Pictures, 1981

'The Ten Commandments', Paramount Pictures, Directed by Cecil B. DeMille, 1956

'Gilligan's Island', Sherwood Schwartz, Columbia Broadcasting System (CBS), Gladysya Productions, United Artists Television, 1964-1967

PHOTO CREDITS:

Chapter 1: Image 1–Moses and Burning Bush Illustration, *Holman Bible*, 1890; Image 2–Split Rock with permission of Penny Caldwell, *God Of The Mountain: True Story Behind The Discoveries At The Real Mount Sinai* (Bridge-Logos Publishers) 2008, (www.splitrockresearch.org); Image 3– Ark of the Covenant, Andrew Bell engraving, 18th Century, *Encyclopedia Britannica 3rd Edition*, 1797: Chapter 4: Image 4 – Holy Family Map, Papyrus Coptic Drawing, Artist Unknown / Jesus In Egypt, Ethiopian Ancient Painting, Zege Peninsula, J. Rankin 2016; Image 5–Axum Stelae, Sherri Rankin, 2012; Image 6: Trumpets of Moses, J. Rankin, 2012; Image 7–Church of St. George, J. Rankin, 2012; Image 8–Fasilides Castle, J. Rankin, 2013; Image 9–Debre Berhan Selassie Church, J. Rankin, 2012; Image 10–Lake Tana Monastery, J. Rankin, 2014: Chapter 5: Image 11–Mary On The Mountain, Tim Moore, 2014; Image 12–Finger of God Rock, J. Rankin, 2012; Image 13–*Kneeling Statuette of King Necho*, (Photo: Brooklyn Museum, 71.11): Chapter 6: Image 14–Tana Kirkos Island, J. Rankin, 2012; Image 15–Jim On Board, Wolson, 2012; Image 16–Jungle Pathway, J. Rankin, 2012; Image 17–Jim Finding

Footholds, Steve Inman, 2012; Image 18 – Point at Footholds, Steve Inman, 2012; Image 19–Measuring the Ark, Tim Moore, 2014; Image 20–Bowl/Pole Holes, J. Rankin, 2012; Image 21–Markings of the Ark, J. Rankin, 2014; Image 22–Kirkos Treasury, Steve Inman, 2013; Image 23–Bronze Bowl, T. Moore, 2014; Image 24–Meat Forks/Meat Hooks, Asgedom Tazeze, 2017; Image 25: Abba and Jim With Book, Tim Moore: Chapter 7: Image 26–Cross In The Bible, Sherri Rankin, 2012: Chapter 8: Image 27–Jesus Book, J. Rankin, 2012; Image 28 – The Book / Translation; Image 29–Prochorus and John, Byzantine Etching, Artist Unknown: Chapter 9: Image 30 – Eagle/Croc – J. Rankin 2012; Image 31 - Cross Of Yared, J. Rankin, 2014; Image 32 - Aba Pointing, Top - Steve Inman, 2013, Bottom – Tim Moore 2014; Chapter 10: Image 33 - Guardian Graveyard, Steve Inman, 2014; Image 34 - Tombs, J. Rankin, 2016: Chapter 11: Image 35 - Pole Holes, J. Rankin, 2012; Image 36 - Center Holes Overview, Tim Moore, 2015; Image 37 - Measuring Offset Footholds, Asgedom Tazeze, 2016; Chapter 12: Image 38 - Tankwa Fisherman, Jim Rankin, 2014; Chapter 13: Image 39 - Guardian With Jim, Kathryn Pearce, Top 2015, Bottom 2016; Image 40 - Ephod Harness, Steve Inman, 2012: Chapter 15: Image 41 - Jim with Sisay, Sue Lytle, 2017; Image 42 – Jim and Sherri Rankin, 2013; Image 43 – Arise and God, J. Rankin, 2014

CPSIA information can be obtained
at www.ICGtesting.com
Printed in the USA
JSHW022046160423
40393JS00001B/15